Ancient Texts and the Bible
Book 8 - Easy Reader Edition

Israel...
Through the Book of Leviticus

Minister 2 Others

Ancient Texts and the Bible
Book 8

Israel...
Through the Book of Leviticus

Easy Reader Edition

Israel... Through the Book of Leviticus
ISBN 978-1-947751-26-2

Ancient texts compiled for this series:

The Bible
King James Version 1769

The Book of Enoch
An English translation by Dr. Laurence,
Archbishop of Cashel,
Formerly Professor of Hebrew at Oxford, 1833

The Book of Jasher
Faithfully translated 1840
from the original Hebrew into English
Published by J.H. Parry & Company 1887

The Book of Jubileees
by R.H. Charles, Oxford: Clarendon Press, 1913

Ancient Texts and the Bible

series include:

Book 1: In The Beginning... From Adam to Noah

Book 2: In The Beginning... From Noah to Abraham

Book 3: In The Beginning... From Abraham to Israel

Book 4: In The Beginning... From Israel to Egypt

Book 5: In The Beginning... From Egypt to Goshen

Book 6: Israel... From Goshen to Sinai

Book 7: Israel... From Sinai to the Tabernacle

Book 8: Israel... Through the Book of Leviticus

Book 9: Israel... Through the Book of Numbers

Book 10: Israel... Through the Book of Joshua

Table of Contents:

Forward

The **Ancient Texts and the Bible** series synchronizes the manuscripts of Enoch, Jasher, and Jubileees into the Bible, making one complete storyline. The books are interwoven using the Torah as the backbone, and the extra-biblical texts as the fleshing out of that backbone.

The eighth book in this series contains the entire book of Leviticus, and part of the book of Jasher chapter 83.

Though the language in the writings have been updated, replacing words like "*thou*" and "*thine*" with words like "*you*" and "*your*", the integrity of the verses remain.

The "*Easy Reader*" edition is for those who just want to read the storyline and enjoy the journey. The stop signs and complex formatting have been removed so one may merely focus upon the story being told.

The *Expanded Edition* of **Ancient Texts and the Bible** was created for the more studious reader. The various manuscripts have the following formatting applied to them in this edition:

the Bible - Regular

THE BOOK OF ENOCH - ALL CAPITALS

the Book of Jasher - Italics

<u>the Book of Jubileees - Underlined</u>

Where one of the extra-biblical texts reiterates the Bible, the phrase is then put in a **bold font**. Where two manuscripts overlap each other exclusive of the Bible, then both fonts are used. For instance, where Jasher and Jubileees intercept, the text is then formatted as *Italics and Underlined*.

The stop sign is another element to the *Expanded Edition* that is not seen in the *Easy Reader*. This image points to contradictions in the content. Printed versions also contain page numbers within the stop sign revealing the page where contradictory information is located, and vice versa. This information was not feasible to place in the e-book versions since the page numbers vary depending on the font size the reader chooses. Following, is an example from each edition:

Easy Reader Edition:

(Leviticus 10:1) *(Jasher 83:6...)*
And *on that day,* **Nadab and Abihu, the** *two* **sons of Aaron, took** either of them his censer, and put fire therein, and put incense thereon, *and brought* and offered **strange fire before the LORD, which he commanded them not**.

Expanded Edition:

(Leviticus 10:1) *(Jasher 83:6...)*
And *on that day,* **Nadab and Abihu, the** *two* **sons of Aaron, took** either of them his censer, and put fire therein, and put incense thereon, *and brought* and offered **strange fire before the LORD, which he commanded them not**.

Whichever you choose, may you ***Enjoy the Journey***!

Leviticus: Chapter One

(Leviticus 1:1)

And the LORD called to Moses, and spoke to him out of the tabernacle of the congregation, saying,

(Leviticus 1:2)

Speak to the children of Israel, and say to them, If any man of you bring an offering to the LORD, you shall bring your offering of the cattle, even of the herd, and of the flock.

(Leviticus 1:3)

If his offering be a burnt sacrifice of the herd, let him offer a male without blemish: he shall offer it of his own voluntary will at the door of the tabernacle of the congregation before the LORD.

(Leviticus 1:4)

And he shall put his hand upon the head of the burnt offering; and it shall be accepted for him to make atonement for him.

(Leviticus 1:5)

And he shall kill the bullock before the LORD: and the priests, Aaron's sons, shall bring the blood, and sprinkle the blood round about upon the altar that is by the door of the tabernacle of the congregation.

(Leviticus 1:6)

And he shall flay the burnt offering, and cut it into his pieces.

(Leviticus 1:7)

And the sons of Aaron the priest shall put fire upon the altar, and lay the wood in order upon the fire:

(Leviticus 1:8)

And the priests, Aaron's sons, shall lay the parts, the head, and the fat, in order upon the wood that is on the fire which is upon the altar:

(Leviticus 1:9)

But his inwards and his legs shall he wash in water: and the priest shall burn all on the altar, to be a burnt sacrifice, an offering made by fire, of a sweet savor to the LORD.

(Leviticus 1:10)

And if his offering be of the flocks, namely, of the sheep, or of the goats, for a burnt sacrifice; he shall bring it a male without blemish.

(Leviticus 1:11)

And he shall kill it on the side of the altar northward before the LORD: and the priests, Aaron's sons, shall sprinkle his blood round about upon the altar.

(Leviticus 1:12)

And he shall cut it into his pieces, with his head and his fat: and the priest shall lay them in order on the wood that is on the fire which is upon the altar:

(Leviticus 1:13)

But he shall wash the inwards and the legs with water: and the priest shall bring it all, and burn it upon the altar: it is a burnt sacrifice, an offering made by fire, of a sweet savor to the LORD.

(Leviticus 1:14)

And if the burnt sacrifice for his offering to the LORD be of fowls, then he shall bring his offering of turtledoves, or of young pigeons.

(Leviticus 1:15)

And the priest shall bring it to the altar, and wring off his head, and burn it on the altar; and the blood thereof shall be wrung out at the side of the altar:

(Leviticus 1:16)

And he shall pluck away his crop with his feathers, and cast it beside the altar on the east part, by the place of the ashes:

(Leviticus 1:17)

And he shall cleave it with the wings thereof, but shall not divide it asunder: and the priest shall burn it upon the altar, upon the wood that is upon the fire: it is a burnt sacrifice, an offering made by fire, of a sweet savor to the LORD.

Leviticus: Chapter Two

(Leviticus 2:1)

And when any will offer a meat offering to the LORD, his offering shall be of fine flour; and he shall pour oil upon it, and put frankincense thereon:

(Leviticus 2:2)

And he shall bring it to Aaron's sons the priests: and he shall take thereout his handful of the flour thereof, and of the oil thereof, with all the frankincense thereof; and the priest shall burn the memorial of it upon the altar, to be an offering made by fire, of a sweet savor to the LORD:

(Leviticus 2:3)

And the remnant of the meat offering shall be Aaron's and his sons': it is a thing most holy of the offerings of the LORD made by fire.

(Leviticus 2:4)

And if you bring an oblation of a meat offering baked in the oven, it shall be unleavened cakes of fine flour mingled with oil, or unleavened wafers anointed with oil.

(Leviticus 2:5)

And if your oblation be a meat offering baked in a pan, it shall be of fine flour unleavened, mingled with oil.

(Leviticus 2:6)

You shall part it in pieces, and pour oil thereon: it is a meat offering.

(Leviticus 2:7)

And if your oblation be a meat offering baked in the frying pan, it shall be made of fine flour with oil.

(Leviticus 2:8)

And you shall bring the meat offering that is made of these things to the LORD: and when it is presented to the priest, he shall bring it to the altar.

(Leviticus 2:9)

And the priest shall take from the meat offering a memorial thereof, and shall burn it upon the altar: it is an offering made by fire, of a sweet savor to the LORD.

(Leviticus 2:10)

And that which is left of the meat offering shall be Aaron's and his sons': it is a thing most holy of the offerings of the LORD made by fire.

(Leviticus 2:11)

No meat offering, which you shall bring to the LORD, shall be made with leaven: for you shall burn no leaven, nor any honey, in any offering of the LORD made by fire.

(Leviticus 2:12)

As for the oblation of the firstfruits, you shall offer them to the LORD: but they shall not be burnt on the altar for a sweet savor.

(Leviticus 2:13)

And every oblation of your meat offering shall you season with salt; neither shall you suffer the salt of the covenant of your God to be lacking from your meat offering: with all your offerings you shall offer salt.

(Leviticus 2:14)

And if you offer a meat offering of your firstfruits to the LORD, you shall offer for the meat offering of your firstfruits green ears of corn dried by the fire, even corn beaten out of full ears.

(Leviticus 2:15)

And you shall put oil upon it, and lay frankincense thereon: it is a meat offering.

(Leviticus 2:16)

And the priest shall burn the memorial of it, part of the beaten corn thereof, and part of the oil thereof, with all the frankincense thereof: it is an offering made by fire to the LORD.

Leviticus: Chapter Three

(Leviticus 3:1)
And if his oblation be a sacrifice of peace offering, if he offer it of the herd; whether it be a male or female, he shall offer it without blemish before the LORD.

(Leviticus 3:2)
And he shall lay his hand upon the head of his offering, and kill it at the door of the tabernacle of the congregation: and Aaron's sons the priests shall sprinkle the blood upon the altar round about.

(Leviticus 3:3)
And he shall offer of the sacrifice of the peace offering an offering made by fire to the LORD; the fat that covers the inwards, and all the fat that is upon the inwards,

(Leviticus 3:4)
And the two kidneys, and the fat that is on them, which is by the flanks, and the caul above the liver, with the kidneys, it shall he take away.

(Leviticus 3:5)
And Aaron's sons shall burn it on the altar upon the burnt sacrifice, which is upon the wood that is on the fire: it is an offering made by fire, of a sweet savor to the LORD.

(Leviticus 3:6)
And if his offering for a sacrifice of peace offering to the

LORD be of the flock; male or female, he shall offer it without blemish.

(Leviticus 3:7)

If he offer a lamb for his offering, then shall he offer it before the LORD.

(Leviticus 3:8)

And he shall lay his hand upon the head of his offering, and kill it before the tabernacle of the congregation: and Aaron's sons shall sprinkle the blood thereof round about upon the altar.

(Leviticus 3:9)

And he shall offer of the sacrifice of the peace offering an offering made by fire to the LORD; the fat thereof, and the whole rump, it shall he take off hard by the backbone; and the fat that covers the inwards, and all the fat that is upon the inwards,

(Leviticus 3:10)

And the two kidneys, and the fat that is upon them, which is by the flanks, and the caul above the liver, with the kidneys, it shall he take away.

(Leviticus 3:11)

And the priest shall burn it upon the altar: it is the food of the offering made by fire to the LORD.

(Leviticus 3:12)

And if his offering be a goat, then he shall offer it before the LORD.

(Leviticus 3:13)

And he shall lay his hand upon the head of it, and kill it before the tabernacle of the congregation: and the sons of Aaron shall sprinkle the blood thereof upon the altar round about.

(Leviticus 3:14)

And he shall offer thereof his offering, even an offering made by fire to the LORD; the fat that covers the inwards, and all the fat that is upon the inwards,

(Leviticus 3:15)

And the two kidneys, and the fat that is upon them, which is by the flanks, and the caul above the liver, with the kidneys, it shall he take away.

(Leviticus 3:16)

And the priest shall burn them upon the altar: it is the food of the offering made by fire for a sweet savor: all the fat is the LORD'S.

(Leviticus 3:17)

It shall be a perpetual statute for your generations throughout all your dwellings, that you eat neither fat nor blood.

Leviticus: Chapter Four

(Leviticus 4:1)
And the LORD spoke to Moses, saying,

(Leviticus 4:2)
Speak to the children of Israel, saying, If a soul shall sin through ignorance against any of the commandments of the LORD concerning things which ought not to be done, and shall do against any of them:

(Leviticus 4:3)
If the priest that is anointed do sin according to the sin of the people; then let him bring for his sin, which he has sinned, a young bullock without blemish to the LORD for a sin offering.

(Leviticus 4:4)
And he shall bring the bullock to the door of the tabernacle of the congregation before the LORD; and shall lay his hand upon the bullock's head, and kill the bullock before the LORD.

(Leviticus 4:5)
And the priest that is anointed shall take of the bullock's blood, and bring it to the tabernacle of the congregation:

(Leviticus 4:6)
And the priest shall dip his finger in the blood, and sprinkle of the blood seven times before the LORD, before the veil of the sanctuary.

(Leviticus 4:7)

And the priest shall put some of the blood upon the horns of the altar of sweet incense before the LORD, which is in the tabernacle of the congregation; and shall pour all the blood of the bullock at the bottom of the altar of the burnt offering, which is at the door of the tabernacle of the congregation.

(Leviticus 4:8)

And he shall take off from it all the fat of the bullock for the sin offering; the fat that covers the inwards, and all the fat that is upon the inwards,

(Leviticus 4:9)

And the two kidneys, and the fat that is upon them, which is by the flanks, and the caul above the liver, with the kidneys, it shall he take away,

(Leviticus 4:10)

As it was taken off from the bullock of the sacrifice of peace offerings: and the priest shall burn them upon the altar of the burnt offering.

(Leviticus 4:11)

And the skin of the bullock, and all his flesh, with his head, and with his legs, and his inwards, and his dung,

(Leviticus 4:12)

Even the whole bullock shall he carry forth without the camp to a clean place, where the ashes are poured out, and burn him on the wood with fire: where the ashes are poured out shall he be burnt.

(Leviticus 4:13)

And if the whole congregation of Israel sin through ignorance, and the thing be hid from the eyes of the assembly, and they have done somewhat against any of the commandments of the LORD concerning things which should not be done, and are guilty;

(Leviticus 4:14)

When the sin, which they have sinned against it, is known, then the congregation shall offer a young bullock for the sin, and bring him before the tabernacle of the congregation.

(Leviticus 4:15)

And the elders of the congregation shall lay their hands upon the head of the bullock before the LORD: and the bullock shall be killed before the LORD.

(Leviticus 4:16)

And the priest that is anointed shall bring of the bullock's blood to the tabernacle of the congregation:

(Leviticus 4:17)

And the priest shall dip his finger in some of the blood, and sprinkle it seven times before the LORD, even before the veil.

(Leviticus 4:18)

And he shall put some of the blood upon the horns of the altar which is before the LORD, that is in the tabernacle of the congregation, and shall pour out all the blood at the bottom of the altar of the burnt offering, which is at the door of the tabernacle of the congregation.

(Leviticus 4:19)

And he shall take all his fat from him, and burn it upon the altar.

(Leviticus 4:20)

And he shall do with the bullock as he did with the bullock for a sin offering, so shall he do with this: and the priest shall make an atonement for them, and it shall be forgiven them.

(Leviticus 4:21)

And he shall carry forth the bullock without the camp, and burn him as he burned the first bullock: it is a sin offering for the congregation.

(Leviticus 4:22)

When a ruler has sinned, and done somewhat through ignorance against any of the commandments of the LORD his God concerning things which should not be done, and is guilty;

(Leviticus 4:23)

Or if his sin, wherein he has sinned, come to his knowledge; he shall bring his offering, a kid of the goats, a male without blemish:

(Leviticus 4:24)

And he shall lay his hand upon the head of the goat, and kill it in the place where they kill the burnt offering before the LORD: it is a sin offering.

(Leviticus 4:25)

And the priest shall take of the blood of the sin offering with his finger, and put it upon the horns of the altar of burnt offering, and shall pour out his blood at the bottom of the altar of burnt offering.

(Leviticus 4:26)

And he shall burn all his fat upon the altar, as the fat of

the sacrifice of peace offerings: and the priest shall make an atonement for him as concerning his sin, and it shall be forgiven him.

(Leviticus 4:27)

And if any one of the common people sin through ignorance, while he does somewhat against any of the commandments of the LORD concerning things which ought not to be done, and be guilty;

(Leviticus 4:28)

Or if his sin, which he has sinned, come to his knowledge: then he shall bring his offering, a kid of the goats, a female without blemish, for his sin which he has sinned.

(Leviticus 4:29)

And he shall lay his hand upon the head of the sin offering, and slay the sin offering in the place of the burnt offering.

(Leviticus 4:30)

And the priest shall take of the blood thereof with his finger, and put it upon the horns of the altar of burnt offering, and shall pour out all the blood thereof at the bottom of the altar.

(Leviticus 4:31)

And he shall take away all the fat thereof, as the fat is taken away from off the sacrifice of peace offerings; and the priest shall burn it upon the altar for a sweet savor to the LORD; and the priest shall make an atonement for him, and it shall be forgiven him.

(Leviticus 4:32)

And if he bring a lamb for a sin offering, he shall bring it a female without blemish.

(Leviticus 4:33)

And he shall lay his hand upon the head of the sin offering, and slay it for a sin offering in the place where they kill the burnt offering.

(Leviticus 4:34)

And the priest shall take of the blood of the sin offering with his finger, and put it upon the horns of the altar of burnt offering, and shall pour out all the blood thereof at the bottom of the altar:

(Leviticus 4:35)

And he shall take away all the fat thereof, as the fat of the lamb is taken away from the sacrifice of the peace offerings; and the priest shall burn them upon the altar, according to the offerings made by fire to the LORD: and the priest shall make an atonement for his sin that he has committed, and it shall be forgiven him.

Leviticus: Chapter Five

(Leviticus 5:1)
And if a soul sin, and hear the voice of swearing, and is a witness, whether he has seen or known of it; if he do not utter it, then he shall bear his iniquity.

(Leviticus 5:2)
Or if a soul touch any unclean thing, whether it be a carcase of an unclean beast, or a carcase of unclean cattle, or the carcase of unclean creeping things, and if it be hidden from him; he also shall be unclean, and guilty.

(Leviticus 5:3)
Or if he touch the uncleanness of man, whatsoever uncleanness it be that a man shall be defiled withal, and it be hid from him; when he knows of it, then he shall be guilty.

(Leviticus 5:4)
Or if a soul swear, pronouncing with his lips to do evil, or to do good, whatsoever it be that a man shall pronounce with an oath, and it be hid from him; when he knows of it, then he shall be guilty in one of these.

(Leviticus 5:5)
And it shall be, when he shall be guilty in one of these things, that he shall confess that he has sinned in that thing:

(Leviticus 5:6)
And he shall bring his trespass offering to the LORD for his sin which he has sinned, a female from the flock, a lamb or a

kid of the goats, for a sin offering; and the priest shall make an atonement for him concerning his sin.

(Leviticus 5:7)

And if he be not able to bring a lamb, then he shall bring for his trespass, which he has committed, two turtledoves, or two young pigeons, to the LORD; one for a sin offering, and the other for a burnt offering.

(Leviticus 5:8)

And he shall bring them to the priest, who shall offer that which is for the sin offering first, and wring off his head from his neck, but shall not divide it asunder:

(Leviticus 5:9)

And he shall sprinkle of the blood of the sin offering upon the side of the altar; and the rest of the blood shall be wrung out at the bottom of the altar: it is a sin offering.

(Leviticus 5:10)

And he shall offer the second for a burnt offering, according to the manner: and the priest shall make an atonement for him for his sin which he has sinned, and it shall be forgiven him.

(Leviticus 5:11)

But if he be not able to bring two turtledoves, or two young pigeons, then he that sinned shall bring for his offering the tenth part of an ephah of fine flour for a sin offering; he shall put no oil upon it, neither shall he put any frankincense thereon: for it is a sin offering.

(Leviticus 5:12)

Then shall he bring it to the priest, and the priest shall take his handful of it, even a memorial thereof, and burn it on the altar, according to the offerings made by fire to the LORD: it is a sin offering.

(Leviticus 5:13)

And the priest shall make an atonement for him as touching his sin that he has sinned in one of these, and it shall be forgiven him: and the remnant shall be the priest's, as a meat offering.

(Leviticus 5:14)

And the LORD spoke to Moses, saying,

(Leviticus 5:15)

If a soul commit a trespass, and sin through ignorance, in the holy things of the LORD; then he shall bring for his trespass to the LORD a ram without blemish out of the flocks, with your estimation by shekels of silver, after the shekel of the sanctuary, for a trespass offering:

(Leviticus 5:16)

And he shall make amends for the harm that he has done in the holy thing, and shall add the fifth part thereto, and give it to the priest: and the priest shall make an atonement for him with the ram of the trespass offering, and it shall be forgiven him.

(Leviticus 5:17)

And if a soul sin, and commit any of these things which are forbidden to be done by the commandments of the LORD; though he knew it not, yet is he guilty, and shall bear his iniquity.

(Leviticus 5:18)

And he shall bring a ram without blemish out of the flock, with your estimation, for a trespass offering, to the priest: and the priest shall make an atonement for him concerning his ignorance wherein he erred and wist it not, and it shall be forgiven him.

(Leviticus 5:19)

It is a trespass offering: he has certainly trespassed against the LORD.

Leviticus: Chapter Six

(Leviticus 6:1)
And the LORD spoke to Moses, saying,

(Leviticus 6:2)
If a soul sin, and commit a trespass against the LORD, and lie to his neighbor in that which was delivered him to keep, or in fellowship, or in a thing taken away by violence, or has deceived his neighbor;

(Leviticus 6:3)
Or have found that which was lost, and lies concerning it, and swears falsely; in any of all these that a man does, sinning therein:

(Leviticus 6:4)
Then it shall be, because he has sinned, and is guilty, that he shall restore that which he took violently away, or the thing which he has deceitfully gotten, or that which was delivered him to keep, or the lost thing which he found,

(Leviticus 6:5)
Or all that about which he has sworn falsely; he shall even restore it in the principal, and shall add the fifth part more thereto, and give it to him to whom it appertains, in the day of his trespass offering.

(Leviticus 6:6)

And he shall bring his trespass offering to the LORD, a ram without blemish out of the flock, with your estimation, for a trespass offering, to the priest:

(Leviticus 6:7)

And the priest shall make an atonement for him before the LORD: and it shall be forgiven him for any thing of all that he has done in trespassing therein.

(Leviticus 6:8)

And the LORD spoke to Moses, saying,

(Leviticus 6:9)

Command Aaron and his sons, saying, This is the law of the burnt offering: It is the burnt offering, because of the burning upon the altar all night to the morning, and the fire of the altar shall be burning in it.

(Leviticus 6:10)

And the priest shall put on his linen garment, and his linen breeches shall he put upon his flesh, and take up the ashes which the fire has consumed with the burnt offering on the altar, and he shall put them beside the altar.

(Leviticus 6:11)

And he shall put off his garments, and put on other garments, and carry forth the ashes without the camp to a clean place.

(Leviticus 6:12)

And the fire upon the altar shall be burning in it; it shall not be put out: and the priest shall burn wood on it every morning, and lay the burnt offering in order upon it; and he shall burn thereon the fat of the peace offerings.

(Leviticus 6:13)
The fire shall ever be burning upon the altar; it shall never go out.

(Leviticus 6:14)
And this is the law of the meat offering: the sons of Aaron shall offer it before the LORD, before the altar.

(Leviticus 6:15)
And he shall take of it his handful, of the flour of the meat offering, and of the oil thereof, and all the frankincense which is upon the meat offering, and shall burn it upon the altar for a sweet savor, even the memorial of it, to the LORD.

(Leviticus 6:16)
And the remainder thereof shall Aaron and his sons eat: with unleavened bread shall it be eaten in the holy place; in the court of the tabernacle of the congregation they shall eat it.

(Leviticus 6:17)
It shall not be baked with leaven. I have given it to them for their portion of my offerings made by fire; it is most holy, as is the sin offering, and as the trespass offering.

(Leviticus 6:18)
All the males among the children of Aaron shall eat of it. It shall be a statute forever in your generations concerning the offerings of the LORD made by fire: every one that touches them shall be holy.

(Leviticus 6:19)
And the LORD spoke to Moses, saying,

(Leviticus 6:20)

This is the offering of Aaron and of his sons, which they shall offer to the LORD in the day when he is anointed; the tenth part of an ephah of fine flour for a meat offering perpetual, half of it in the morning, and half thereof at night.

(Leviticus 6:21)

In a pan it shall be made with oil; and when it is baked, you shall bring it in: and the baked pieces of the meat offering shall you offer for a sweet savor to the LORD.

(Leviticus 6:22)

And the priest of his sons that is anointed in his stead shall offer it: it is a statute forever to the LORD; it shall be wholly burnt.

(Leviticus 6:23)

For every meat offering for the priest shall be wholly burnt: it shall not be eaten.

(Leviticus 6:24)

And the LORD spoke to Moses, saying,

(Leviticus 6:25)

Speak to Aaron and to his sons, saying, This is the law of the sin offering: In the place where the burnt offering is killed shall the sin offering be killed before the LORD: it is most holy.

(Leviticus 6:26)

The priest that offers it for sin shall eat it: in the holy place shall it be eaten, in the court of the tabernacle of the congregation.

(Leviticus 6:27)

Whatsoever shall touch the flesh thereof shall be holy: and when there is sprinkled of the blood thereof upon any garment, you shall wash that whereon it was sprinkled in the holy place.

(Leviticus 6:28)

But the earthen vessel wherein it is sodden shall be broken: and if it be sodden in a brazen pot, it shall be both scoured, and rinsed in water.

(Leviticus 6:29)

All the males among the priests shall eat thereof: it is most holy.

(Leviticus 6:30)

And no sin offering, whereof any of the blood is brought into the tabernacle of the congregation to reconcile withal in the holy place, shall be eaten: it shall be burnt in the fire.

Leviticus: Chapter Seven

(Leviticus 7:1)
Likewise this is the law of the trespass offering: it is most holy.

(Leviticus 7:2)
In the place where they kill the burnt offering shall they kill the trespass offering: and the blood thereof shall he sprinkle round about upon the altar.

(Leviticus 7:3)
And he shall offer of it all the fat thereof; the rump, and the fat that covers the inwards,

(Leviticus 7:4)
And the two kidneys, and the fat that is on them, which is by the flanks, and the caul that is above the liver, with the kidneys, it shall he take away:

(Leviticus 7:5)
And the priest shall burn them upon the altar for an offering made by fire to the LORD: it is a trespass offering.

(Leviticus 7:6)
Every male among the priests shall eat thereof: it shall be eaten in the holy place: it is most holy.

(Leviticus 7:7)
As the sin offering is, so is the trespass offering: there is one law for them: the priest that makes atonement therewith shall have it.

(Leviticus 7:8)

And the priest that offers any man's burnt offering, even the priest shall have to himself the skin of the burnt offering which he has offered.

(Leviticus 7:9)

And all the meat offering that is baked in the oven, and all that is dressed in the frying pan, and in the pan, shall be the priest's that offers it.

(Leviticus 7:10)

And every meat offering, mingled with oil, and dry, shall all the sons of Aaron have, one as much as another.

(Leviticus 7:11)

And this is the law of the sacrifice of peace offerings, which he shall offer to the LORD.

(Leviticus 7:12)

If he offer it for a thanksgiving, then he shall offer with the sacrifice of thanksgiving unleavened cakes mingled with oil, and unleavened wafers anointed with oil, and cakes mingled with oil, of fine flour, fried.

(Leviticus 7:13)

Besides the cakes, he shall offer for his offering leavened bread with the sacrifice of thanksgiving of his peace offerings.

(Leviticus 7:14)

And of it he shall offer one out of the whole oblation for an heave offering to the LORD, and it shall be the priest's that sprinkles the blood of the peace offerings.

(Leviticus 7:15)

And the flesh of the sacrifice of his peace offerings for thanksgiving shall be eaten the same day that it is offered; he shall not leave any of it until the morning.

(Leviticus 7:16)

But if the sacrifice of his offering be a vow, or a voluntary offering, it shall be eaten the same day that he offers his sacrifice: and on the morrow also the remainder of it shall be eaten:

(Leviticus 7:17)

But the remainder of the flesh of the sacrifice on the third day shall be burnt with fire.

(Leviticus 7:18)

And if any of the flesh of the sacrifice of his peace offerings be eaten at all on the third day, it shall not be accepted, neither shall it be imputed to him that offers it: it shall be an abomination, and the soul that eats of it shall bear his iniquity.

(Leviticus 7:19)

And the flesh that touches any unclean thing shall not be eaten; it shall be burnt with fire: and as for the flesh, all that be clean shall eat thereof.

(Leviticus 7:20)

But the soul that eats of the flesh of the sacrifice of peace offerings, that pertain to the LORD, having his uncleanness upon him, even that soul shall be cut off from his people.

(Leviticus 7:21)

Moreover the soul that shall touch any unclean thing, as the uncleanness of man, or any unclean beast, or any abominable unclean thing, and eat of the flesh of the sacrifice of peace offerings, which pertain to the LORD, even that soul shall be cut off from his people.

(Leviticus 7:22)
And the LORD spoke to Moses, saying,

(Leviticus 7:23)
Speak to the children of Israel, saying, You shall eat no manner of fat, of ox, or of sheep, or of goat.

(Leviticus 7:24)
And the fat of the beast that dies of itself, and the fat of that which is torn with beasts, may be used in any other use: but you shall in no wise eat of it.

(Leviticus 7:25)
For whosoever eats the fat of the beast, of which men offer an offering made by fire to the LORD, even the soul that eats it shall be cut off from his people.

(Leviticus 7:26)
Moreover you shall eat no manner of blood, whether it be of fowl or of beast, in any of your dwellings.

(Leviticus 7:27)
Whatsoever soul it be that eats any manner of blood, even that soul shall be cut off from his people.

(Leviticus 7:28)
And the LORD spoke to Moses, saying,

(Leviticus 7:29)

Speak to the children of Israel, saying, He that offers the sacrifice of his peace offerings to the LORD shall bring his oblation to the LORD of the sacrifice of his peace offerings.

(Leviticus 7:30)

His own hands shall bring the offerings of the LORD made by fire, the fat with the breast, it shall he bring, that the breast may be waved for a wave offering before the LORD.

(Leviticus 7:31)

And the priest shall burn the fat upon the altar: but the breast shall be Aaron's and his sons'.

(Leviticus 7:32)

And the right shoulder shall you give to the priest for an heave offering of the sacrifices of your peace offerings.

(Leviticus 7:33)

He among the sons of Aaron, that offers the blood of the peace offerings, and the fat, shall have the right shoulder for his part.

(Leviticus 7:34)

For the wave breast and the heave shoulder have I taken of the children of Israel from off the sacrifices of their peace offerings, and have given them to Aaron the priest and to his sons by a statute forever from among the children of Israel.

(Leviticus 7:35)

This is the portion of the anointing of Aaron, and of the anointing of his sons, out of the offerings of the LORD made by fire, in the day when he presented them to minister to the LORD in the priest's office;

(Leviticus 7:36)

Which the LORD commanded to be given them of the children of Israel, in the day that he anointed them, by a statute forever throughout their generations.

(Leviticus 7:37)

This is the law of the burnt offering, of the meat offering, and of the sin offering, and of the trespass offering, and of the consecrations, and of the sacrifice of the peace offerings;

(Leviticus 7:38)

Which the LORD commanded Moses in mount Sinai, in the day that he commanded the children of Israel to offer their oblations to the LORD, in the wilderness of Sinai.

Leviticus: Chapter Eight

(Leviticus 8:1)
And the LORD spoke to Moses, saying,

(Leviticus 8:2)
Take Aaron and his sons with him, and the garments, and the anointing oil, and a bullock for the sin offering, and two rams, and a basket of unleavened bread;

(Leviticus 8:3)
And gather all the congregation together to the door of the tabernacle of the congregation.

(Leviticus 8:4)
And Moses did as the LORD commanded him; and the assembly was gathered together to the door of the tabernacle of the congregation.

(Leviticus 8:5)
And Moses said to the congregation, This is the thing which the LORD commanded to be done.

(Leviticus 8:6)
And Moses brought Aaron and his sons, and washed them with water.

(Leviticus 8:7)
And he put upon him the coat, and girded him with the girdle, and clothed him with the robe, and put the ephod upon him,

and he girded him with the curious girdle of the ephod, and bound it to him therewith.

(Leviticus 8:8)

And he put the breastplate upon him: also he put in the breastplate the Urim and the Thummim.

(Leviticus 8:9)

And he put the mitre upon his head; also upon the mitre, even upon his forefront, did he put the golden plate, the holy crown; as the LORD commanded Moses.

(Leviticus 8:10)

And Moses took the anointing oil, and anointed the tabernacle and all that was therein, and sanctified them.

(Leviticus 8:11)

And he sprinkled thereof upon the altar seven times, and anointed the altar and all his vessels, both the laver and his foot, to sanctify them.

(Leviticus 8:12)

And he poured of the anointing oil upon Aaron's head, and anointed him, to sanctify him.

(Leviticus 8:13)

And Moses brought Aaron's sons, and put coats upon them, and girded them with girdles, and put bonnets upon them; as the LORD commanded Moses.

(Leviticus 8:14)

And he brought the bullock for the sin offering: and Aaron and his sons laid their hands upon the head of the bullock for the sin offering.

(Leviticus 8:15)

And he slew it; and Moses took the blood, and put it upon the horns of the altar round about with his finger, and purified the altar, and poured the blood at the bottom of the altar, and sanctified it, to make reconciliation upon it.

(Leviticus 8:16)

And he took all the fat that was upon the inwards, and the caul above the liver, and the two kidneys, and their fat, and Moses burned it upon the altar.

(Leviticus 8:17)

But the bullock, and his hide, his flesh, and his dung, he burnt with fire without the camp; as the LORD commanded Moses.

(Leviticus 8:18)

And he brought the ram for the burnt offering: and Aaron and his sons laid their hands upon the head of the ram.

(Leviticus 8:19)

And he killed it; and Moses sprinkled the blood upon the altar round about.

(Leviticus 8:20)

And he cut the ram into pieces; and Moses burnt the head, and the pieces, and the fat.

(Leviticus 8:21)

And he washed the inwards and the legs in water; and Moses burnt the whole ram upon the altar: it was a burnt sacrifice for a sweet savor, and an offering made by fire to the LORD; as the LORD commanded Moses.

(Leviticus 8:22)

And he brought the other ram, the ram of consecration: and Aaron and his sons laid their hands upon the head of the ram.

(Leviticus 8:23)

And he slew it; and Moses took of the blood of it, and put it upon the tip of Aaron's right ear, and upon the thumb of his right hand, and upon the great toe of his right foot.

(Leviticus 8:24)

And he brought Aaron's sons, and Moses put of the blood upon the tip of their right ear, and upon the thumbs of their right hands, and upon the great toes of their right feet: and Moses sprinkled the blood upon the altar round about.

(Leviticus 8:25)

And he took the fat, and the rump, and all the fat that was upon the inwards, and the caul above the liver, and the two kidneys, and their fat, and the right shoulder:

(Leviticus 8:26)

And out of the basket of unleavened bread, that was before the LORD, he took one unleavened cake, and a cake of oiled bread, and one wafer, and put them on the fat, and upon the right shoulder:

(Leviticus 8:27)

And he put all upon Aaron's hands, and upon his sons' hands, and waved them for a wave offering before the LORD.

(Leviticus 8:28)

And Moses took them from off their hands, and burnt them on the altar upon the burnt offering: they were consecrations for a sweet savor: it is an offering made by fire to the LORD.

(Leviticus 8:29)

And Moses took the breast, and waved it for a wave offering before the LORD: for of the ram of consecration it was Moses' part; as the LORD commanded Moses.

(Leviticus 8:30)

And Moses took of the anointing oil, and of the blood which was upon the altar, and sprinkled it upon Aaron, and upon his garments, and upon his sons, and upon his sons' garments with him; and sanctified Aaron, and his garments, and his sons, and his sons' garments with him.

(Leviticus 8:31)

And Moses said to Aaron and to his sons, Boil the flesh at the door of the tabernacle of the congregation: and there eat it with the bread that is in the basket of consecrations, as I commanded, saying, Aaron and his sons shall eat it.

(Leviticus 8:32)

And that which remains of the flesh and of the bread shall you burn with fire.

(Leviticus 8:33)

And you shall not go out of the door of the tabernacle of the congregation in seven days, until the days of your consecration be at an end: for seven days shall he consecrate you.

(Leviticus 8:34)

As he has done this day, so the LORD has commanded to do, to make an atonement for you.

(Leviticus 8:35)

Therefore shall you abide at the door of the tabernacle of the congregation day and night seven days, and keep the charge of the LORD, that you die not: for so I am commanded.

(Leviticus 8:36)

So Aaron and his sons did all things which the LORD commanded by the hand of Moses.

Leviticus: Chapter Nine

(Leviticus 9:1) (Jasher 83:5...)

And it came to pass on the eighth day, that Moses called Aaron and his sons, and the elders of Israel;

(Leviticus 9:2)

And he said to Aaron, Take you a young calf for a sin offering, and a ram for a burnt offering, without blemish, and offer them before the LORD.

(Leviticus 9:3)

And to the children of Israel you shall speak, saying, Take you a kid of the goats for a sin offering; and a calf and a lamb, both of the first year, without blemish, for a burnt offering;

(Leviticus 9:4)

Also a bullock and a ram for peace offerings, to sacrifice before the LORD; and a meat offering mingled with oil: for to day the LORD will appear to you.

(Leviticus 9:5)

And they brought that which Moses commanded before the tabernacle of the congregation: and all the congregation drew near and stood before the LORD.

(Leviticus 9:6)

And Moses said, This is the thing which the LORD commanded that you should do: and the glory of the LORD shall appear to you.

(Leviticus 9:7)

And Moses said to Aaron, Go to the altar, and offer your sin offering, and your burnt offering, and make an atonement for yourself, and for the people: and offer the offering of the people, and make an atonement for them; as the LORD commanded.

(...Jasher 83:5)

And they brought the burnt offering and the sin offering for themselves and the children of Israel, as the Lord had commanded Moses.

(Leviticus 9:8)

Aaron therefore went to the altar, and slew the calf of the sin offering, which was for himself.

(Leviticus 9:9)

And the sons of Aaron brought the blood to him: and he dipped his finger in the blood, and put it upon the horns of the altar, and poured out the blood at the bottom of the altar:

(Leviticus 9:10)

But the fat, and the kidneys, and the caul above the liver of the sin offering, he burnt upon the altar; as the LORD commanded Moses.

(Leviticus 9:11)

And the flesh and the hide he burnt with fire without the camp.

(Leviticus 9:12)

And he slew the burnt offering; and Aaron's sons presented to him the blood, which he sprinkled round about upon the altar.

(Leviticus 9:13)

And they presented the burnt offering to him, with the pieces thereof, and the head: and he burnt them upon the altar.

(Leviticus 9:14)

And he did wash the inwards and the legs, and burnt them upon the burnt offering on the altar.

(Leviticus 9:15)

And he brought the people's offering, and took the goat, which was the sin offering for the people, and slew it, and offered it for sin, as the first.

(Leviticus 9:16)

And he brought the burnt offering, and offered it according to the manner.

(Leviticus 9:17)

And he brought the meat offering, and took an handful thereof, and burnt it upon the altar, beside the burnt sacrifice of the morning.

(Leviticus 9:18)

He slew also the bullock and the ram for a sacrifice of peace offerings, which was for the people: and Aaron's sons presented to him the blood, which he sprinkled upon the altar round about,

(Leviticus 9:19)

And the fat of the bullock and of the ram, the rump, and that which covers the inwards, and the kidneys, and the caul above the liver:

(Leviticus 9:20)

And they put the fat upon the breasts, and he burnt the fat upon the altar:

(Leviticus 9:21)

And the breasts and the right shoulder Aaron waved for a wave offering before the LORD; as Moses commanded.

(Leviticus 9:22)

And Aaron lifted up his hand toward the people, and blessed them, and came down from offering of the sin offering, and the burnt offering, and peace offerings.

(Leviticus 9:23)

And Moses and Aaron went into the tabernacle of the congregation, and came out, and blessed the people: and the glory of the LORD appeared to all the people.

(Leviticus 9:24)

And there came a fire out from before the LORD, and consumed upon the altar the burnt offering and the fat: which when all the people saw, they shouted, and fell on their faces.

Leviticus: Chapter Ten

(Leviticus 10:1) (Jasher 83:6...)

And on that day, Nadab and Abihu, the two sons of Aaron, took either of them his censer, and put fire therein, and put incense thereon, and brought and offered strange fire before the LORD, which he commanded them not.

(Leviticus 10:2) (...Jasher 83:6)

And there went out fire from the LORD, and devoured them, and they died before the LORD on that day.

(Leviticus 10:3)

Then Moses said to Aaron, This is it that the LORD spoke, saying, I will be sanctified in them that come nigh me, and before all the people I will be glorified. And Aaron held his peace.

(Leviticus 10:4)

And Moses called Mishael and Elzaphan, the sons of Uzziel the uncle of Aaron, and said to them, Come near, carry your brothers from before the sanctuary out of the camp.

(Leviticus 10:5)

So they went near, and carried them in their coats out of the camp; as Moses had said.

(Leviticus 10:6)

And Moses said to Aaron, and to Eleazar and to Ithamar, his sons, Uncover not your heads, neither rend your clothes; lest you die, and lest wrath come upon all the people: but let your brothers, the whole house of Israel, bewail the burning which the LORD has kindled.

(Leviticus 10:7)
And you shall not go out from the door of the tabernacle of the congregation, lest you die: for the anointing oil of the LORD is upon you. And they did according to the word of Moses.

(Leviticus 10:8)
And the LORD spoke to Aaron, saying,

(Leviticus 10:9)
Do not drink wine nor strong drink, you, nor your sons with you, when you go into the tabernacle of the congregation, lest you die: it shall be a statute forever throughout your generations:

(Leviticus 10:10)
And that you may put difference between holy and unholy, and between unclean and clean;

(Leviticus 10:11)
And that you may teach the children of Israel all the statutes which the LORD has spoken to them by the hand of Moses.

(Leviticus 10:12)
And Moses spoke to Aaron, and to Eleazar and to Ithamar, his sons that were left, Take the meat offering that remains of the offerings of the LORD made by fire, and eat it without leaven beside the altar: for it is most holy:

(Leviticus 10:13)
And you shall eat it in the holy place, because it is your due, and your sons' due, of the sacrifices of the LORD made by fire:

for so I am commanded.

(Leviticus 10:14)

And the wave breast and heave shoulder shall you eat in a clean place; you, and your sons, and your daughters with you: for they be your due, and your sons' due, which are given out of the sacrifices of peace offerings of the children of Israel.

(Leviticus 10:15)

The heave shoulder and the wave breast shall they bring with the offerings made by fire of the fat, to wave it for a wave offering before the LORD; and it shall be your, and your sons' with you, by a statute forever; as the LORD has commanded.

(Leviticus 10:16)

And Moses diligently sought the goat of the sin offering, and, behold, it was burnt: and he was angry with Eleazar and Ithamar, the sons of Aaron which were left alive, saying,

(Leviticus 10:17)

Why have you not eaten the sin offering in the holy place, seeing it is most holy, and God has given it you to bear the iniquity of the congregation, to make atonement for them before the LORD?

(Leviticus 10:18)

Behold, the blood of it was not brought in within the holy place: you should indeed have eaten it in the holy place, as I commanded.

(Leviticus 10:19)

And Aaron said to Moses, Behold, this day have they offered their sin offering and their burnt offering before the LORD; and such things have befallen me: and if I had eaten the sin offering to day, should it have been accepted in the sight of the LORD?

(Leviticus 10:20)
And when Moses heard that, he was content.

(Jasher 83:7)
Then on the day when Moses had completed to erect the sanctuary, the princes of the children of Israel began to bring their offerings before the Lord for the dedication of the altar.

(Jasher 83:8)
And they brought up their offerings each prince for one day, a prince each day for twelve days.

(Jasher 83:9)
And all the offerings which they brought, each man in his day, one silver charger weighing one hundred and thirty shekels, one silver bowl of seventy shekels after the shekel of the sanctuary, both of them full of fine flour, mingled with oil for a meat offering.

(Jasher 83:10)
One spoon, weighing ten shekels of gold, full of incense.

(Jasher 83:11)
One young bullock, one ram, one lamb of the first year for a burnt offering.

(Jasher 83:12)
And one kid of the goats for a sin offering.

(Jasher 83:13)
And for a sacrifice of peace offering, two oxen, five rams, five he-goats, five lambs of a year old.

(Jasher 83:14)
Thus did the twelve princes of Israel day by day, each man in his day.

(Jasher 83:15)
And it was after this, in the thirteenth day of the month, that Moses commanded the children of Israel to observe the Passover.

(Jasher 83:16)
And the children of Israel kept the Passover in its season in the fourteenth day of the month, as the Lord had commanded Moses, so did the children of Israel.

Leviticus: Chapter Eleven

(Leviticus 11:1)
And the LORD spoke to Moses and to Aaron, saying to them,

(Leviticus 11:2)
Speak to the children of Israel, saying, These are the beasts which you shall eat among all the beasts that are on the earth.

(Leviticus 11:3)
Whatsoever parts the hoof, and is cloven-footed, and chews the cud, among the beasts, that shall you eat.

(Leviticus 11:4)
Nevertheless these shall you not eat of them that chew the cud, or of them that divides the hoof: as the camel, because he chews the cud, but divides not the hoof; he is unclean to you.

(Leviticus 11:5)
And the coney, because he chews the cud, but divides not the hoof; he is unclean to you.

(Leviticus 11:6)
And the hare, because he chews the cud, but divides not the hoof; he is unclean to you.

(Leviticus 11:7)
And the swine, though he divides the hoof, and be cloven-footed, yet he chews not the cud; he is unclean to you.

(Leviticus 11:8)
Of their flesh shall you not eat, and their carcase shall you not touch; they are unclean to you.

(Leviticus 11:9)
These shall you eat of all that are in the waters: whatsoever has fins and scales in the waters, in the seas, and in the rivers, them shall you eat.

(Leviticus 11:10)
And all that have not fins and scales in the seas, and in the rivers, of all that move in the waters, and of any living thing which is in the waters, they shall be an abomination to you:

(Leviticus 11:11)
They shall be even an abomination to you; you shall not eat of their flesh, but you shall have their carcases in abomination.

(Leviticus 11:12)
Whatsoever has no fins nor scales in the waters, that shall be an abomination to you.

(Leviticus 11:13)
And these are they which you shall have in abomination among the fowls; they shall not be eaten, they are an abomination: the eagle, and the ossifrage, and the ospray,

(Leviticus 11:14)
And the vulture, and the kite after his kind;

(Leviticus 11:15)
Every raven after his kind;

(Leviticus 11:16)
And the owl, and the night hawk, and the cuckow, and the hawk after his kind,

(Leviticus 11:17)
And the little owl, and the cormorant, and the great owl,

(Leviticus 11:18)
And the swan, and the pelican, and the gier eagle,

(Leviticus 11:19)
And the stork, the heron after her kind, and the lapwing, and the bat.

(Leviticus 11:20)
All fowls that creep, going upon all four, shall be an abomination to you.

(Leviticus 11:21)
Yet these may you eat of every flying creeping thing that goes upon all four, which have legs above their feet, to leap withal upon the earth;

(Leviticus 11:22)
Even these of them you may eat; the locust after his kind, and the bald locust after his kind, and the beetle after his kind, and the grasshopper after his kind.

(Leviticus 11:23)
But all other flying creeping things, which have four feet, shall be an abomination to you.

(Leviticus 11:24)
And for these you shall be unclean: whosoever touches the carcase of them shall be unclean until the even.

(Leviticus 11:25)
And whosoever bears ought of the carcase of them shall wash his clothes, and be unclean until the even.

(Leviticus 11:26)
The carcases of every beast which divides the hoof, and is not cloven-footed, nor chews the cud, are unclean to you: every one that touches them shall be unclean.

(Leviticus 11:27)
And whatsoever goes upon his paws, among all manner of beasts that go on all four, those are unclean to you: whoso touches their carcase shall be unclean until the even.

(Leviticus 11:28)
And he that bears the carcase of them shall wash his clothes, and be unclean until the even: they are unclean to you.

(Leviticus 11:29)
These also shall be unclean to you among the creeping things that creep upon the earth; the weasel, and the mouse, and the tortoise after his kind,

(Leviticus 11:30)
And the ferret, and the chameleon, and the lizard, and the snail, and the mole.

(Leviticus 11:31)
These are unclean to you among all that creep: whosoever

does touch them, when they be dead, shall be unclean until the even.

(Leviticus 11:32)

And upon whatsoever any of them, when they are dead, does fall, it shall be unclean; whether it be any vessel of wood, or raiment, or skin, or sack, whatsoever vessel it be, wherein any work is done, it must be put into water, and it shall be unclean until the even; so it shall be cleansed.

(Leviticus 11:33)

And every earthen vessel, whereinto any of them falls, whatsoever is in it shall be unclean; and you shall break it.

(Leviticus 11:34)

Of all meat which may be eaten, that on which such water comes shall be unclean: and all drink that may be drunk in every such vessel shall be unclean.

(Leviticus 11:35)

And every thing whereupon any part of their carcase falls shall be unclean; whether it be oven, or ranges for pots, they shall be broken down: for they are unclean, and shall be unclean to you.

(Leviticus 11:36)

Nevertheless a fountain or pit, wherein there is plenty of water, shall be clean: but that which touches their carcase shall be unclean.

(Leviticus 11:37)

And if any part of their carcase fall upon any sowing seed which is to be sown, it shall be clean.

(Leviticus 11:38)

But if any water be put upon the seed, and any part of their carcase fall thereon, it shall be unclean to you.

(Leviticus 11:39)

And if any beast, of which you may eat, die; he that touches the carcase thereof shall be unclean until the even.

(Leviticus 11:40)

And he that eats of the carcase of it shall wash his clothes, and be unclean until the even: he also that bears the carcase of it shall wash his clothes, and be unclean until the even.

(Leviticus 11:41)

And every creeping thing that creeps upon the earth shall be an abomination; it shall not be eaten.

(Leviticus 11:42)

Whatsoever goes upon the belly, and whatsoever goes upon all four, or whatsoever has more feet among all creeping things that creep upon the earth, them you shall not eat; for they are an abomination.

(Leviticus 11:43)

You shall not make yourselves abominable with any creeping thing that creeps, neither shall you make yourselves unclean with them, that you should be defiled thereby.

(Leviticus 11:44)

For I am the LORD your God: you shall therefore sanctify yourselves, and you shall be holy; for I am holy: neither shall you defile yourselves with any manner of creeping thing that creeps upon the earth.

(Leviticus 11:45)

For I am the LORD that brings you up out of the land of Egypt, to be your God: you shall therefore be holy, for I am holy.

(Leviticus 11:46)

This is the law of the beasts, and of the fowl, and of every living creature that moves in the waters, and of every creature that creeps upon the earth:

(Leviticus 11:47)

To make a difference between the unclean and the clean, and between the beast that may be eaten and the beast that may not be eaten.

Leviticus: Chapter Twelve

(Leviticus 12:1)
And the LORD spoke to Moses, saying,

(Leviticus 12:2)
Speak to the children of Israel, saying, If a woman have conceived seed, and born a man child: then she shall be unclean seven days; according to the days of the separation for her infirmity shall she be unclean.

(Leviticus 12:3)
And in the eighth day the flesh of his foreskin shall be circumcised.

(Leviticus 12:4)
And she shall then continue in the blood of her purifying three and thirty days; she shall touch no hallowed thing, nor come into the sanctuary, until the days of her purifying be fulfilled.

(Leviticus 12:5)
But if she bear a maid child, then she shall be unclean two weeks, as in her separation: and she shall continue in the blood of her purifying threescore and six days.

(Leviticus 12:6)
And when the days of her purifying are fulfilled, for a son, or for a daughter, she shall bring a lamb of the first year for a burnt offering, and a young pigeon, or a turtledove, for a sin offering, to the door of the tabernacle of the congregation, to the priest:

(Leviticus 12:7)

Who shall offer it before the LORD, and make an atonement for her; and she shall be cleansed from the issue of her blood. This is the law for her that has born a male or a female.

(Leviticus 12:8)

And if she be not able to bring a lamb, then she shall bring two turtles, or two young pigeons; the one for the burnt offering, and the other for a sin offering: and the priest shall make an atonement for her, and she shall be clean.

Leviticus: Chapter Thirteen

(Leviticus 13:1)
And the LORD spoke to Moses and Aaron, saying,

(Leviticus 13:2)
When a man shall have in the skin of his flesh a rising, a scab, or bright spot, and it be in the skin of his flesh like the plague of leprosy; then he shall be brought to Aaron the priest, or to one of his sons the priests:

(Leviticus 13:3)
And the priest shall look on the plague in the skin of the flesh: and when the hair in the plague is turned white, and the plague in sight be deeper than the skin of his flesh, it is a plague of leprosy: and the priest shall look on him, and pronounce him unclean.

(Leviticus 13:4)
If the bright spot be white in the skin of his flesh, and in sight be not deeper than the skin, and the hair thereof be not turned white; then the priest shall shut up him that has the plague seven days:

(Leviticus 13:5)
And the priest shall look on him the seventh day: and, behold, if the plague in his sight be at a stay, and the plague spread not in the skin; then the priest shall shut him up seven days more:

(Leviticus 13:6)

And the priest shall look on him again the seventh day: and, behold, if the plague be somewhat dark, and the plague spread not in the skin, the priest shall pronounce him clean: it is but a scab: and he shall wash his clothes, and be clean.

(Leviticus 13:7)

But if the scab spread much abroad in the skin, after that he has been seen of the priest for his cleansing, he shall be seen of the priest again:

(Leviticus 13:8)

And if the priest see that, behold, the scab spreads in the skin, then the priest shall pronounce him unclean: it is a leprosy.

(Leviticus 13:9)

When the plague of leprosy is in a man, then he shall be brought to the priest;

(Leviticus 13:10)

And the priest shall see him: and, behold, if the rising be white in the skin, and it have turned the hair white, and there be quick raw flesh in the rising;

(Leviticus 13:11)

It is an old leprosy in the skin of his flesh, and the priest shall pronounce him unclean, and shall not shut him up: for he is unclean.

(Leviticus 13:12)

And if a leprosy break out abroad in the skin, and the leprosy cover all the skin of him that has the plague from his head even to his foot, wheresoever the priest looks;

(Leviticus 13:13)
Then the priest shall consider: and, behold, if the leprosy have covered all his flesh, he shall pronounce him clean that has the plague: it is all turned white: he is clean.

(Leviticus 13:14)
But when raw flesh appears in him, he shall be unclean.

(Leviticus 13:15)
And the priest shall see the raw flesh, and pronounce him to be unclean: for the raw flesh is unclean: it is a leprosy.

(Leviticus 13:16)
Or if the raw flesh turn again, and be changed to white, he shall come to the priest;

(Leviticus 13:17)
And the priest shall see him: and, behold, if the plague be turned into white; then the priest shall pronounce him clean that has the plague: he is clean.

(Leviticus 13:18)
The flesh also, in which, even in the skin thereof, was a boil, and is healed,

(Leviticus 13:19)
And in the place of the boil there be a white rising, or a bright spot, white, and somewhat reddish, and it be showed to the priest;

(Leviticus 13:20)
And if, when the priest sees it, behold, it be in sight lower than the skin, and the hair thereof be turned white; the priest shall

pronounce him unclean: it is a plague of leprosy broken out of the boil.

(Leviticus 13:21)

But if the priest look on it, and, behold, there be no white hairs therein, and if it be not lower than the skin, but be somewhat dark; then the priest shall shut him up seven days:

(Leviticus 13:22)

And if it spread much abroad in the skin, then the priest shall pronounce him unclean: it is a plague.

(Leviticus 13:23)

But if the bright spot stay in his place, and spread not, it is a burning boil; and the priest shall pronounce him clean.

(Leviticus 13:24)

Or if there be any flesh, in the skin whereof there is a hot burning, and the quick flesh that burns have a white bright spot, somewhat reddish, or white;

(Leviticus 13:25)

Then the priest shall look upon it: and, behold, if the hair in the bright spot be turned white, and it be in sight deeper than the skin; it is a leprosy broken out of the burning: wherefore the priest shall pronounce him unclean: it is the plague of leprosy.

(Leviticus 13:26)

But if the priest look on it, and, behold, there be no white hair in the bright spot, and it be no lower than the other skin, but be somewhat dark; then the priest shall shut him up seven days:

(Leviticus 13:27)

And the priest shall look upon him the seventh day: and if it be spread much abroad in the skin, then the priest shall pronounce him unclean: it is the plague of leprosy.

(Leviticus 13:28)

And if the bright spot stay in his place, and spread not in the skin, but it be somewhat dark; it is a rising of the burning, and the priest shall pronounce him clean: for it is an inflammation of the burning.

(Leviticus 13:29)

If a man or woman have a plague upon the head or the beard;

(Leviticus 13:30)

Then the priest shall see the plague: and, behold, if it be in sight deeper than the skin; and there be in it a yellow thin hair; then the priest shall pronounce him unclean: it is a dry scall, even a leprosy upon the head or beard.

(Leviticus 13:31)

And if the priest look on the plague of the scall, and, behold, it be not in sight deeper than the skin, and that there is no black hair in it; then the priest shall shut up him that has the plague of the scall seven days:

(Leviticus 13:32)

And in the seventh day the priest shall look on the plague: and, behold, if the scall spread not, and there be in it no yellow hair, and the scall be not in sight deeper than the skin;

(Leviticus 13:33)

He shall be shaven, but the scall shall he not shave; and the priest shall shut up him that has the scall seven days more:

(Leviticus 13:34)

And in the seventh day the priest shall look on the scall: and, behold, if the scall be not spread in the skin, nor be in sight deeper than the skin; then the priest shall pronounce him clean: and he shall wash his clothes, and be clean.

(Leviticus 13:35)

But if the scall spread much in the skin after his cleansing;

(Leviticus 13:36)

Then the priest shall look on him: and, behold, if the scall be spread in the skin, the priest shall not seek for yellow hair; he is unclean.

(Leviticus 13:37)

But if the scall be in his sight at a stay, and that there is black hair grown up therein; the scall is healed, he is clean: and the priest shall pronounce him clean.

(Leviticus 13:38)

If a man also or a woman have in the skin of their flesh bright spots, even white bright spots;

(Leviticus 13:39)

Then the priest shall look: and, behold, if the bright spots in the skin of their flesh be darkish white; it is a freckled spot that grows in the skin; he is clean.

(Leviticus 13:40)

And the man whose hair is fallen off his head, he is bald; yet is he clean.

(Leviticus 13:41)

And he that has his hair fallen off from the part of his head toward his face, he is forehead bald: yet is he clean.

(Leviticus 13:42)
And if there be in the bald head, or bald forehead, a white reddish sore; it is a leprosy sprung up in his bald head, or his bald forehead.

(Leviticus 13:43)
Then the priest shall look upon it: and, behold, if the rising of the sore be white reddish in his bald head, or in his bald forehead, as the leprosy appears in the skin of the flesh;

(Leviticus 13:44)
He is a leprous man, he is unclean: the priest shall pronounce him utterly unclean; his plague is in his head.

(Leviticus 13:45)
And the leper in whom the plague is, his clothes shall be rent, and his head bare, and he shall put a covering upon his upper lip, and shall cry, Unclean, unclean.

(Leviticus 13:46)
All the days wherein the plague shall be in him he shall be defiled; he is unclean: he shall dwell alone; without the camp shall his habitation be.

(Leviticus 13:47)
The garment also that the plague of leprosy is in, whether it be a woolen garment, or a linen garment;

(Leviticus 13:48)
Whether it be in the warp, or woof; of linen, or of woolen; whether in a skin, or in any thing made of skin;

(Leviticus 13:49)

And if the plague be greenish or reddish in the garment, or in the skin, either in the warp, or in the woof, or in any thing of skin; it is a plague of leprosy, and shall be showed to the priest:

(Leviticus 13:50)

And the priest shall look upon the plague, and shut up it that has the plague seven days:

(Leviticus 13:51)

And he shall look on the plague on the seventh day: if the plague be spread in the garment, either in the warp, or in the woof, or in a skin, or in any work that is made of skin; the plague is a fretting leprosy; it is unclean.

(Leviticus 13:52)

He shall therefore burn that garment, whether warp or woof, in woolen or in linen, or any thing of skin, wherein the plague is: for it is a fretting leprosy; it shall be burnt in the fire.

(Leviticus 13:53)

And if the priest shall look, and, behold, the plague be not spread in the garment, either in the warp, or in the woof, or in any thing of skin;

(Leviticus 13:54)

Then the priest shall command that they wash the thing wherein the plague is, and he shall shut it up seven days more:

(Leviticus 13:55)

And the priest shall look on the plague, after that it is washed: and, behold, if the plague have not changed his color, and the plague be not spread; it is unclean; you shall burn it in the fire; it is fret inward, whether it be bare within or without.

(Leviticus 13:56)

And if the priest look, and, behold, the plague be somewhat dark after the washing of it; then he shall rend it out of the garment, or out of the skin, or out of the warp, or out of the woof:

(Leviticus 13:57)

And if it appear still in the garment, either in the warp, or in the woof, or in any thing of skin; it is a spreading plague: you shall burn that wherein the plague is with fire.

(Leviticus 13:58)

And the garment, either warp, or woof, or whatsoever thing of skin it be, which you shall wash, if the plague be departed from them, then it shall be washed the second time, and shall be clean.

(Leviticus 13:59)

This is the law of the plague of leprosy in a garment of woolen or linen, either in the warp, or woof, or any thing of skins, to pronounce it clean, or to pronounce it unclean.

Leviticus: Chapter Fourteen

(Leviticus 14:1)
And the LORD spoke to Moses, saying,

(Leviticus 14:2)
This shall be the law of the leper in the day of his cleansing: He shall be brought to the priest:

(Leviticus 14:3)
And the priest shall go forth out of the camp; and the priest shall look, and, behold, if the plague of leprosy be healed in the leper;

(Leviticus 14:4)
Then shall the priest command to take for him that is to be cleansed two birds alive and clean, and cedar wood, and scarlet, and hyssop:

(Leviticus 14:5)
And the priest shall command that one of the birds be killed in an earthen vessel over running water:

(Leviticus 14:6)
As for the living bird, he shall take it, and the cedar wood, and the scarlet, and the hyssop, and shall dip them and the living bird in the blood of the bird that was killed over the running water:

(Leviticus 14:7)
And he shall sprinkle upon him that is to be cleansed from the

leprosy seven times, and shall pronounce him clean, and shall let the living bird loose into the open field.

(Leviticus 14:8)

And he that is to be cleansed shall wash his clothes, and shave off all his hair, and wash himself in water, that he may be clean: and after that he shall come into the camp, and shall tarry abroad out of his tent seven days.

(Leviticus 14:9)

But it shall be on the seventh day, that he shall shave all his hair off his head and his beard and his eyebrows, even all his hair he shall shave off: and he shall wash his clothes, also he shall wash his flesh in water, and he shall be clean.

(Leviticus 14:10)

And on the eighth day he shall take two he lambs without blemish, and one ewe lamb of the first year without blemish, and three tenth deals of fine flour for a meat offering, mingled with oil, and one log of oil.

(Leviticus 14:11)

And the priest that makes him clean shall present the man that is to be made clean, and those things, before the LORD, at the door of the tabernacle of the congregation:

(Leviticus 14:12)

And the priest shall take one he lamb, and offer him for a trespass offering, and the log of oil, and wave them for a wave offering before the LORD:

(Leviticus 14:13)

And he shall slay the lamb in the place where he shall kill the sin offering and the burnt offering, in the holy place: for as the sin offering is the priest's, so is the trespass offering: it is most holy:

(Leviticus 14:14)

And the priest shall take some of the blood of the trespass offering, and the priest shall put it upon the tip of the right ear of him that is to be cleansed, and upon the thumb of his right hand, and upon the great toe of his right foot:

(Leviticus 14:15)

And the priest shall take some of the log of oil, and pour it into the palm of his own left hand:

(Leviticus 14:16)

And the priest shall dip his right finger in the oil that is in his left hand, and shall sprinkle of the oil with his finger seven times before the LORD:

(Leviticus 14:17)

And of the rest of the oil that is in his hand shall the priest put upon the tip of the right ear of him that is to be cleansed, and upon the thumb of his right hand, and upon the great toe of his right foot, upon the blood of the trespass offering:

(Leviticus 14:18)

And the remnant of the oil that is in the priest's hand he shall pour upon the head of him that is to be cleansed: and the priest shall make an atonement for him before the LORD.

(Leviticus 14:19)

And the priest shall offer the sin offering, and make an atonement for him that is to be cleansed from his uncleanness; and afterward he shall kill the burnt offering:

(Leviticus 14:20)

And the priest shall offer the burnt offering and the meat offering upon the altar: and the priest shall make an atonement for him, and he shall be clean.

(Leviticus 14:21)

And if he be poor, and cannot get so much; then he shall take one lamb for a trespass offering to be waved, to make an atonement for him, and one tenth deal of fine flour mingled with oil for a meat offering, and a log of oil;

(Leviticus 14:22)

And two turtledoves, or two young pigeons, such as he is able to get; and the one shall be a sin offering, and the other a burnt offering.

(Leviticus 14:23)

And he shall bring them on the eighth day for his cleansing to the priest, to the door of the tabernacle of the congregation, before the LORD.

(Leviticus 14:24)

And the priest shall take the lamb of the trespass offering, and the log of oil, and the priest shall wave them for a wave offering before the LORD:

(Leviticus 14:25)

And he shall kill the lamb of the trespass offering, and the priest shall take some of the blood of the trespass offering, and put it upon the tip of the right ear of him that is to be cleansed, and upon the thumb of his right hand, and upon the great toe of his right foot:

(Leviticus 14:26)

And the priest shall pour of the oil into the palm of his own left hand:

(Leviticus 14:27)

And the priest shall sprinkle with his right finger some of the oil that is in his left hand seven times before the LORD:

(Leviticus 14:28)

And the priest shall put of the oil that is in his hand upon the tip of the right ear of him that is to be cleansed, and upon the thumb of his right hand, and upon the great toe of his right foot, upon the place of the blood of the trespass offering:

(Leviticus 14:29)

And the rest of the oil that is in the priest's hand he shall put upon the head of him that is to be cleansed, to make an atonement for him before the LORD.

(Leviticus 14:30)

And he shall offer the one of the turtledoves, or of the young pigeons, such as he can get;

(Leviticus 14:31)

Even such as he is able to get, the one for a sin offering, and the other for a burnt offering, with the meat offering: and the priest shall make an atonement for him that is to be cleansed before the LORD.

(Leviticus 14:32)

This is the law of him in whom is the plague of leprosy, whose hand is not able to get that which pertains to his cleansing.

(Leviticus 14:33)
And the LORD spoke to Moses and to Aaron, saying,

(Leviticus 14:34)
When you be come into the land of Canaan, which I give to you for a possession, and I put the plague of leprosy in a house of the land of your possession;

(Leviticus 14:35)
And he that owns the house shall come and tell the priest, saying, It seems to me there is as it were a plague in the house:

(Leviticus 14:36)
Then the priest shall command that they empty the house, before the priest go into it to see the plague, that all that is in the house be not made unclean: and afterward the priest shall go in to see the house:

(Leviticus 14:37)
And he shall look on the plague, and, behold, if the plague be in the walls of the house with hollow streaks, greenish or reddish, which in sight are lower than the wall;

(Leviticus 14:38)
Then the priest shall go out of the house to the door of the house, and shut up the house seven days:

(Leviticus 14:39)
And the priest shall come again the seventh day, and shall look: and, behold, if the plague be spread in the walls of the house;

(Leviticus 14:40)
Then the priest shall command that they take away the stones

in which the plague is, and they shall cast them into an unclean place without the city:

(Leviticus 14:41)

And he shall cause the house to be scraped within round about, and they shall pour out the dust that they scrape off without the city into an unclean place:

(Leviticus 14:42)

And they shall take other stones, and put them in the place of those stones; and he shall take other mortar, and shall plaster the house.

(Leviticus 14:43)

And if the plague come again, and break out in the house, after that he has taken away the stones, and after he has scraped the house, and after it is plastered;

(Leviticus 14:44)

Then the priest shall come and look, and, behold, if the plague be spread in the house, it is a fretting leprosy in the house: it is unclean.

(Leviticus 14:45)

And he shall break down the house, the stones of it, and the timber thereof, and all the mortar of the house; and he shall carry them forth out of the city into an unclean place.

(Leviticus 14:46)

Moreover he that goes into the house all the while that it is shut up shall be unclean until the even.

(Leviticus 14:47)

And he that lies in the house shall wash his clothes; and he that eats in the house shall wash his clothes.

(Leviticus 14:48)

And if the priest shall come in, and look upon it, and, behold, the plague has not spread in the house, after the house was plastered: then the priest shall pronounce the house clean, because the plague is healed.

(Leviticus 14:49)

And he shall take to cleanse the house two birds, and cedar wood, and scarlet, and hyssop:

(Leviticus 14:50)

And he shall kill the one of the birds in an earthen vessel over running water:

(Leviticus 14:51)

And he shall take the cedar wood, and the hyssop, and the scarlet, and the living bird, and dip them in the blood of the slain bird, and in the running water, and sprinkle the house seven times:

(Leviticus 14:52)

And he shall cleanse the house with the blood of the bird, and with the running water, and with the living bird, and with the cedar wood, and with the hyssop, and with the scarlet:

(Leviticus 14:53)

But he shall let go the living bird out of the city into the open fields, and make an atonement for the house: and it shall be clean.

(Leviticus 14:54)

This is the law for all manner of plague of leprosy, and scall,

(Leviticus 14:55)

And for the leprosy of a garment, and of a house,

(Leviticus 14:56)

And for a rising, and for a scab, and for a bright spot:

(Leviticus 14:57)

To teach when it is unclean, and when it is clean: this is the law of leprosy.

Leviticus: Chapter Fifteen

(Leviticus 15:1)
And the LORD spoke to Moses and to Aaron, saying,

(Leviticus 15:2)
Speak to the children of Israel, and say to them, When any man has a running issue out of his flesh, because of his issue he is unclean.

(Leviticus 15:3)
And this shall be his uncleanness in his issue: whether his flesh run with his issue, or his flesh be stopped from his issue, it is his uncleanness.

(Leviticus 15:4)
Every bed, whereon he lies that has the issue, is unclean: and every thing, whereon he sits, shall be unclean.

(Leviticus 15:5)
And whosoever touches his bed shall wash his clothes, and bathe himself in water, and be unclean until the even.

(Leviticus 15:6)
And he that sits on any thing whereon he sat that has the issue shall wash his clothes, and bathe himself in water, and be unclean until the even.

(Leviticus 15:7)
And he that touches the flesh of him that has the issue shall

wash his clothes, and bathe himself in water, and be unclean until the even.

(Leviticus 15:8)

And if he that has the issue spit upon him that is clean; then he shall wash his clothes, and bathe himself in water, and be unclean until the even.

(Leviticus 15:9)

And what saddle soever he rides upon that has the issue shall be unclean.

(Leviticus 15:10)

And whosoever touches any thing that was under him shall be unclean until the even: and he that bears any of those things shall wash his clothes, and bathe himself in water, and be unclean until the even.

(Leviticus 15:11)

And whomsoever he touches that has the issue, and has not rinsed his hands in water, he shall wash his clothes, and bathe himself in water, and be unclean until the even.

(Leviticus 15:12)

And the vessel of earth, that he touches which has the issue, shall be broken: and every vessel of wood shall be rinsed in water.

(Leviticus 15:13)

And when he that has an issue is cleansed of his issue; then he shall number to himself seven days for his cleansing, and wash his clothes, and bathe his flesh in running water, and shall be clean.

(Leviticus 15:14)

And on the eighth day he shall take to him two turtledoves, or two young pigeons, and come before the LORD to the door of the tabernacle of the congregation, and give them to the priest:

(Leviticus 15:15)

And the priest shall offer them, the one for a sin offering, and the other for a burnt offering; and the priest shall make an atonement for him before the LORD for his issue.

(Leviticus 15:16)

And if any man's seed of copulation go out from him, then he shall wash all his flesh in water, and be unclean until the even.

(Leviticus 15:17)

And every garment, and every skin, whereon is the seed of copulation, shall be washed with water, and be unclean until the even.

(Leviticus 15:18)

The woman also with whom man shall lie with seed of copulation, they shall both bathe themselves in water, and be unclean until the even.

(Leviticus 15:19)

And if a woman have an issue, and her issue in her flesh be blood, she shall be put apart seven days: and whosoever touches her shall be unclean until the even.

(Leviticus 15:20)

And every thing that she lies upon in her separation shall be unclean: every thing also that she sits upon shall be unclean.

(Leviticus 15:21)

And whosoever touches her bed shall wash his clothes, and bathe himself in water, and be unclean until the even.

(Leviticus 15:22)

And whosoever touches any thing that she sat upon shall wash his clothes, and bathe himself in water, and be unclean until the even.

(Leviticus 15:23)

And if it be on her bed, or on any thing whereon she sits, when he touches it, he shall be unclean until the even.

(Leviticus 15:24)

And if any man lie with her at all, and her flowers be upon him, he shall be unclean seven days; and all the bed whereon he lies shall be unclean.

(Leviticus 15:25)

And if a woman have an issue of her blood many days out of the time of her separation, or if it run beyond the time of her separation; all the days of the issue of her uncleanness shall be as the days of her separation: she shall be unclean.

(Leviticus 15:26)

Every bed whereon she lies all the days of her issue shall be to her as the bed of her separation: and whatsoever she sits upon shall be unclean, as the uncleanness of her separation.

(Leviticus 15:27)

And whosoever touches those things shall be unclean, and shall wash his clothes, and bathe himself in water, and be unclean until the even.

(Leviticus 15:28)

But if she be cleansed of her issue, then she shall number to herself seven days, and after that she shall be clean.

(Leviticus 15:29)

And on the eighth day she shall take to her two turtles, or two young pigeons, and bring them to the priest, to the door of the tabernacle of the congregation.

(Leviticus 15:30)

And the priest shall offer the one for a sin offering, and the other for a burnt offering; and the priest shall make an atonement for her before the LORD for the issue of her uncleanness.

(Leviticus 15:31)

Thus shall you separate the children of Israel from their uncleanness; that they die not in their uncleanness, when they defile my tabernacle that is among them.

(Leviticus 15:32)

This is the law of him that has an issue, and of him whose seed goes from him, and is defiled therewith;

(Leviticus 15:33)

And of her that is sick of her flowers, and of him that has an issue, of the man, and of the woman, and of him that lies with her that is unclean.

Leviticus: Chapter Sixteen

(Leviticus 16:1)
And the LORD spoke to Moses after the death of the two sons of Aaron, when they offered before the LORD, and died;

(Leviticus 16:2)
And the LORD said to Moses, Speak to Aaron your brother, that he come not at all times into the holy place within the veil before the mercy seat, which is upon the ark; that he die not: for I will appear in the cloud upon the mercy seat.

(Leviticus 16:3)
Thus shall Aaron come into the holy place: with a young bullock for a sin offering, and a ram for a burnt offering.

(Leviticus 16:4)
He shall put on the holy linen coat, and he shall have the linen breeches upon his flesh, and shall be girded with a linen girdle, and with the linen mitre shall he be attired: these are holy garments; therefore shall he wash his flesh in water, and so put them on.

(Leviticus 16:5)
And he shall take of the congregation of the children of Israel two kids of the goats for a sin offering, and one ram for a burnt offering.

(Leviticus 16:6)
And Aaron shall offer his bullock of the sin offering, which is

for himself, and make an atonement for himself, and for his house.

(Leviticus 16:7)
And he shall take the two goats, and present them before the LORD at the door of the tabernacle of the congregation.

(Leviticus 16:8)
And Aaron shall cast lots upon the two goats; one lot for the LORD, and the other lot for the scapegoat.

(Leviticus 16:9)
And Aaron shall bring the goat upon which the LORD'S lot fell, and offer him for a sin offering.

(Leviticus 16:10)
But the goat, on which the lot fell to be the scapegoat, shall be presented alive before the LORD, to make an atonement with him, and to let him go for a scapegoat into the wilderness.

(Leviticus 16:11)
And Aaron shall bring the bullock of the sin offering, which is for himself, and shall make an atonement for himself, and for his house, and shall kill the bullock of the sin offering which is for himself:

(Leviticus 16:12)
And he shall take a censer full of burning coals of fire from off the altar before the LORD, and his hands full of sweet incense beaten small, and bring it within the veil:

(Leviticus 16:13)
And he shall put the incense upon the fire before the LORD,

that the cloud of the incense may cover the mercy seat that is upon the testimony, that he die not:

(Leviticus 16:14)
And he shall take of the blood of the bullock, and sprinkle it with his finger upon the mercy seat eastward; and before the mercy seat shall he sprinkle of the blood with his finger seven times.

(Leviticus 16:15)
Then shall he kill the goat of the sin offering, that is for the people, and bring his blood within the veil, and do with that blood as he did with the blood of the bullock, and sprinkle it upon the mercy seat, and before the mercy seat:

(Leviticus 16:16)
And he shall make an atonement for the holy place, because of the uncleanness of the children of Israel, and because of their transgressions in all their sins: and so shall he do for the tabernacle of the congregation, that remains among them in the midst of their uncleanness.

(Leviticus 16:17)
And there shall be no man in the tabernacle of the congregation when he goes in to make an atonement in the holy place, until he come out, and have made an atonement for himself, and for his household, and for all the congregation of Israel.

(Leviticus 16:18)
And he shall go out to the altar that is before the LORD, and make an atonement for it; and shall take of the blood of the bullock, and of the blood of the goat, and put it upon the horns of the altar round about.

(Leviticus 16:19)

And he shall sprinkle of the blood upon it with his finger seven times, and cleanse it, and hallow it from the uncleanness of the children of Israel.

(Leviticus 16:20)

And when he has made an end of reconciling the holy place, and the tabernacle of the congregation, and the altar, he shall bring the live goat:

(Leviticus 16:21)

And Aaron shall lay both his hands upon the head of the live goat, and confess over him all the iniquities of the children of Israel, and all their transgressions in all their sins, putting them upon the head of the goat, and shall send him away by the hand of a fit man into the wilderness:

(Leviticus 16:22)

And the goat shall bear upon him all their iniquities to a land not inhabited: and he shall let go the goat in the wilderness.

(Leviticus 16:23)

And Aaron shall come into the tabernacle of the congregation, and shall put off the linen garments, which he put on when he went into the holy place, and shall leave them there:

(Leviticus 16:24)

And he shall wash his flesh with water in the holy place, and put on his garments, and come forth, and offer his burnt offering, and the burnt offering of the people, and make an atonement for himself, and for the people.

(Leviticus 16:25)

And the fat of the sin offering shall he burn upon the altar.

(Leviticus 16:26)

And he that let go the goat for the scapegoat shall wash his clothes, and bathe his flesh in water, and afterward come into the camp.

(Leviticus 16:27)

And the bullock for the sin offering, and the goat for the sin offering, whose blood was brought in to make atonement in the holy place, shall one carry forth without the camp; and they shall burn in the fire their skins, and their flesh, and their dung.

(Leviticus 16:28)

And he that burns them shall wash his clothes, and bathe his flesh in water, and afterward he shall come into the camp.

(Leviticus 16:29)

And this shall be a statute forever to you: that in the seventh month, on the tenth day of the month, you shall afflict your souls, and do no work at all, whether it be one of your own country, or a stranger that sojourns among you:

(Leviticus 16:30)

For on that day shall the priest make an atonement for you, to cleanse you, that you may be clean from all your sins before the LORD.

(Leviticus 16:31)

It shall be a sabbath of rest to you, and you shall afflict your souls, by a statute forever.

(Leviticus 16:32)

And the priest, whom he shall anoint, and whom he shall consecrate to minister in the priest's office in his father's stead, shall make the atonement, and shall put on the linen clothes, even the holy garments:

(Leviticus 16:33)
And he shall make an atonement for the holy sanctuary, and he shall make an atonement for the tabernacle of the congregation, and for the altar, and he shall make an atonement for the priests, and for all the people of the congregation.

(Leviticus 16:34)
And this shall be an everlasting statute to you, to make an atonement for the children of Israel for all their sins once a year. And he did as the LORD commanded Moses.

Leviticus: Chapter Seventeen

(Leviticus 17:1)
And the LORD spoke to Moses, saying,

(Leviticus 17:2)
Speak to Aaron, and to his sons, and to all the children of Israel, and say to them; This is the thing which the LORD has commanded, saying,

(Leviticus 17:3)
What man soever there be of the house of Israel, that kills an ox, or lamb, or goat, in the camp, or that kills it out of the camp,

(Leviticus 17:4)
And brings it not to the door of the tabernacle of the congregation, to offer an offering to the LORD before the tabernacle of the LORD; blood shall be imputed to that man; he has shed blood; and that man shall be cut off from among his people:

(Leviticus 17:5)
To the end that the children of Israel may bring their sacrifices, which they offer in the open field, even that they may bring them to the LORD, to the door of the tabernacle of the congregation, to the priest, and offer them for peace offerings to the LORD.

(Leviticus 17:6)
And the priest shall sprinkle the blood upon the altar of the

LORD at the door of the tabernacle of the congregation, and burn the fat for a sweet savor to the LORD.

(Leviticus 17:7)

And they shall no more offer their sacrifices to devils, after whom they have gone a whoring. This shall be a statute forever to them throughout their generations.

(Leviticus 17:8)

And you shall say to them, Whatsoever man there be of the house of Israel, or of the strangers which sojourn among you, that offers a burnt offering or sacrifice,

(Leviticus 17:9)

And brings it not to the door of the tabernacle of the congregation, to offer it to the LORD; even that man shall be cut off from among his people.

(Leviticus 17:10)

And whatsoever man there be of the house of Israel, or of the strangers that sojourn among you, that eats any manner of blood; I will even set my face against that soul that eats blood, and will cut him off from among his people.

(Leviticus 17:11)

For the life of the flesh is in the blood: and I have given it to you upon the altar to make an atonement for your souls: for it is the blood that makes an atonement for the soul.

(Leviticus 17:12)

Therefore I said to the children of Israel, No soul of you shall eat blood, neither shall any stranger that sojourns among you eat blood.

(Leviticus 17:13)

And whatsoever man there be of the children of Israel, or of the strangers that sojourn among you, which hunt and catch any beast or fowl that may be eaten; he shall even pour out the blood thereof, and cover it with dust.

(Leviticus 17:14)

For it is the life of all flesh; the blood of it is for the life thereof: therefore I said to the children of Israel, You shall eat the blood of no manner of flesh: for the life of all flesh is the blood thereof: whosoever eats it shall be cut off.

(Leviticus 17:15)

And every soul that eats that which died of itself, or that which was torn with beasts, whether it be one of your own country, or a stranger, he shall both wash his clothes, and bathe himself in water, and be unclean until the even: then shall he be clean.

(Leviticus 17:16)

But if he wash them not, nor bathe his flesh; then he shall bear his iniquity.

Leviticus: Chapter Eighteen

(Leviticus 18:1)
And the LORD spoke to Moses, saying,

(Leviticus 18:2)
Speak to the children of Israel, and say to them, I am the LORD your God.

(Leviticus 18:3)
After the doings of the land of Egypt, wherein you dwelt, shall you not do: and after the doings of the land of Canaan, whither I bring you, shall you not do: neither shall you walk in their ordinances.

(Leviticus 18:4)
You shall do my judgments, and keep mine ordinances, to walk therein: I am the LORD your God.

(Leviticus 18:5)
You shall therefore keep my statutes, and my judgments: which if a man do, he shall live in them: I am the LORD.

(Leviticus 18:6)
None of you shall approach to any that is near of kin to him, to uncover their nakedness: I am the LORD.

(Leviticus 18:7)
The nakedness of your father, or the nakedness of your mother, shall you not uncover: she is your mother; you shall not uncover her nakedness.

(Leviticus 18:8)

The nakedness of your father's wife shall you not uncover: it is your father's nakedness.

(Leviticus 18:9)

The nakedness of your sister, the daughter of your father, or daughter of your mother, whether she be born at home, or born abroad, even their nakedness you shall not uncover.

(Leviticus 18:10)

The nakedness of your son's daughter, or of your daughter's daughter, even their nakedness you shall not uncover: for theirs is your own nakedness.

(Leviticus 18:11)

The nakedness of your father's wife's daughter, begotten of your father, she is your sister, you shall not uncover her nakedness.

(Leviticus 18:12)

You shall not uncover the nakedness of your father's sister: she is your father's near kinswoman.

(Leviticus 18:13)

You shall not uncover the nakedness of your mother's sister: for she is your mother's near kinswoman.

(Leviticus 18:14)

You shall not uncover the nakedness of your father's brother, you shall not approach to his wife: she is your aunt.

(Leviticus 18:15)

You shall not uncover the nakedness of your daughter in law: she is your son's wife; you shall not uncover her nakedness.

(Leviticus 18:16)

You shall not uncover the nakedness of your brother's wife: it is your brother's nakedness.

(Leviticus 18:17)

You shall not uncover the nakedness of a woman and her daughter, neither shall you take her son's daughter, or her daughter's daughter, to uncover her nakedness; for they are her near kinswomen: it is wickedness.

(Leviticus 18:18)

Neither shall you take a wife to her sister, to vex her, to uncover her nakedness, beside the other in her life time.

(Leviticus 18:19)

Also you shall not approach to a woman to uncover her nakedness, as long as she is put apart for her uncleanness.

(Leviticus 18:20)

Moreover you shall not lie carnally with your neighbor's wife, to defile yourself with her.

(Leviticus 18:21)

And you shall not let any of your seed pass through the fire to Molech, neither shall you profane the name of your God: I am the LORD.

(Leviticus 18:22)

You shall not lie with mankind, as with womankind: it is abomination.

(Leviticus 18:23)

Neither shall you lie with any beast to defile yourself therewith: neither shall any woman stand before a beast to lie down thereto: it is confusion.

(Leviticus 18:24)

Defile not you yourselves in any of these things: for in all these the nations are defiled which I cast out before you:

(Leviticus 18:25)

And the land is defiled: therefore I do visit the iniquity thereof upon it, and the land itself vomits out her inhabitants.

(Leviticus 18:26)

You shall therefore keep my statutes and my judgments, and shall not commit any of these abominations; neither any of your own nation, nor any stranger that sojourns among you:

(Leviticus 18:27)

(For all these abominations have the men of the land done, which were before you, and the land is defiled;)

(Leviticus 18:28)

That the land spew not you out also, when you defile it, as it spewed out the nations that were before you.

(Leviticus 18:29)

For whosoever shall commit any of these abominations, even the souls that commit them shall be cut off from among their people.

(Leviticus 18:30)

Therefore shall you keep mine ordinance, that you commit not any one of these abominable customs, which were committed before you, and that you defile not yourselves therein: I am the LORD your God.

Leviticus: Chapter Nineteen

(Leviticus 19:1)
And the LORD spoke to Moses, saying,

(Leviticus 19:2)
Speak to all the congregation of the children of Israel, and say to them, You shall be holy: for I the LORD your God am holy.

(Leviticus 19:3)
You shall fear every man his mother, and his father, and keep my sabbaths: I am the LORD your God.

(Leviticus 19:4)
Turn you not to idols, nor make to yourselves molten gods: I am the LORD your God.

(Leviticus 19:5)
And if you offer a sacrifice of peace offerings to the LORD, you shall offer it at your own will.

(Leviticus 19:6)
It shall be eaten the same day you offer it, and on the morrow: and if ought remain until the third day, it shall be burnt in the fire.

(Leviticus 19:7)
And if it be eaten at all on the third day, it is abominable; it shall not be accepted.

(Leviticus 19:8)

Therefore every one that eats it shall bear his iniquity, because he has profaned the hallowed thing of the LORD: and that soul shall be cut off from among his people.

(Leviticus 19:9)

And when you reap the harvest of your land, you shall not wholly reap the corners of your field, neither shall you gather the gleanings of your harvest.

(Leviticus 19:10)

And you shall not glean your vineyard, neither shall you gather every grape of your vineyard; you shall leave them for the poor and stranger: I am the LORD your God.

(Leviticus 19:11)

You shall not steal, neither deal falsely, neither lie one to another.

(Leviticus 19:12)

And you shall not swear by my name falsely, neither shall you profane the name of your God: I am the LORD.

(Leviticus 19:13)

You shall not defraud your neighbor, neither rob him: the wages of him that is hired shall not abide with you all night until the morning.

(Leviticus 19:14)

You shall not curse the deaf, nor put a stumbling block before the blind, but shall fear your God: I am the LORD.

(Leviticus 19:15)

You shall do no unrighteousness in judgment: you shall not

respect the person of the poor, nor honor the person of the mighty: but in righteousness shall you judge your neighbor.

(Leviticus 19:16)
You shall not go up and down as a talebearer among your people: neither shall you stand against the blood of your neighbor: I am the LORD.

(Leviticus 19:17)
You shall not hate your brother in your heart: you shall in any wise rebuke your neighbor, and not suffer sin upon him.

(Leviticus 19:18)
You shall not avenge, nor bear any grudge against the children of your people, but you shall love your neighbor as yourself: I am the LORD.

(Leviticus 19:19)
You shall keep my statutes. You shall not let your cattle gender with a diverse kind: you shall not sow your field with mingled seed: neither shall a garment mingled of linen and woolen come upon you.

(Leviticus 19:20)
And whosoever lies carnally with a woman, that is a bondmaid, betrothed to an husband, and not at all redeemed, nor freedom given her; she shall be scourged; they shall not be put to death, because she was not free.

(Leviticus 19:21)
And he shall bring his trespass offering to the LORD, to the door of the tabernacle of the congregation, even a ram for a trespass offering.

(Leviticus 19:22)

And the priest shall make an atonement for him with the ram of the trespass offering before the LORD for his sin which he has done: and the sin which he has done shall be forgiven him.

(Leviticus 19:23)

And when you shall come into the land, and shall have planted all manner of trees for food, then you shall count the fruit thereof as uncircumcised: three years shall it be as uncircumcised to you: it shall not be eaten of.

(Leviticus 19:24)

But in the fourth year all the fruit thereof shall be holy to praise the LORD withal.

(Leviticus 19:25)

And in the fifth year shall you eat of the fruit thereof, that it may yield to you the increase thereof: I am the LORD your God.

(Leviticus 19:26)

You shall not eat any thing with the blood: neither shall you use enchantment, nor observe times.

(Leviticus 19:27)

You shall not round the corners of your heads, neither shall you mar the corners of your beard.

(Leviticus 19:28)

You shall not make any cuttings in your flesh for the dead, nor print any marks upon you: I am the LORD.

(Leviticus 19:29)

Do not prostitute your daughter, to cause her to be a whore; lest the land fall to whoredom, and the land become full of wickedness.

(Leviticus 19:30)

You shall keep my sabbaths, and reverence my sanctuary: I am the LORD.

(Leviticus 19:31)

Regard not them that have familiar spirits, neither seek after wizards, to be defiled by them: I am the LORD your God.

(Leviticus 19:32)

You shall rise up before the hoary head, and honor the face of the old man, and fear your God: I am the LORD.

(Leviticus 19:33)

And if a stranger sojourn with you in your land, you shall not vex him.

(Leviticus 19:34)

But the stranger that dwells with you shall be to you as one born among you, and you shall love him as yourself; for you were strangers in the land of Egypt: I am the LORD your God.

(Leviticus 19:35)

You shall do no unrighteousness in judgment, in meteyard, in weight, or in measure.

(Leviticus 19:36)

Just balances, just weights, a just ephah, and a just hin, shall you have: I am the LORD your God, which brought you out of the land of Egypt.

(Leviticus 19:37)
Therefore shall you observe all my statutes, and all my judgments, and do them: I am the LORD.

Leviticus: Chapter Twenty

(Leviticus 20:1)
And the LORD spoke to Moses, saying,

(Leviticus 20:2)
Again, you shall say to the children of Israel, Whosoever he be of the children of Israel, or of the strangers that sojourn in Israel, that gives any of his seed to Molech; he shall surely be put to death: the people of the land shall stone him with stones.

(Leviticus 20:3)
And I will set my face against that man, and will cut him off from among his people; because he has given of his seed to Molech, to defile my sanctuary, and to profane my holy name.

(Leviticus 20:4)
And if the people of the land do any ways hide their eyes from the man, when he gives of his seed to Molech, and kill him not:

(Leviticus 20:5)
Then I will set my face against that man, and against his family, and will cut him off, and all that go a whoring after him, to commit whoredom with Molech, from among their people.

(Leviticus 20:6)
And the soul that turns after such as have familiar spirits, and after wizards, to go a whoring after them, I will even set my

face against that soul, and will cut him off from among his people.

(Leviticus 20:7)
Sanctify yourselves therefore, and be you holy: for I am the LORD your God.

(Leviticus 20:8)
And you shall keep my statutes, and do them: I am the LORD which sanctify you.

(Leviticus 20:9)
For every one that curses his father or his mother shall be surely put to death: he has cursed his father or his mother; his blood shall be upon him.

(Leviticus 20:10)
And the man that commits adultery with another man's wife, even he that commits adultery with his neighbor's wife, the adulterer and the adulteress shall surely be put to death.

(Leviticus 20:11)
And the man that lies with his father's wife has uncovered his father's nakedness: both of them shall surely be put to death; their blood shall be upon them.

(Leviticus 20:12)
And if a man lie with his daughter in law, both of them shall surely be put to death: they have wrought confusion; their blood shall be upon them.

(Leviticus 20:13)
If a man also lies with mankind, as he lies with a woman, both of them have committed an abomination: they shall surely be

put to death; their blood shall be upon them.

(Leviticus 20:14)
And if a man take a wife and her mother, it is wickedness: they shall be burnt with fire, both he and they; that there be no wickedness among you.

(Leviticus 20:15)
And if a man lies with a beast, he shall surely be put to death: and you shall slay the beast.

(Leviticus 20:16)
And if a woman approach to any beast, and lie down thereto, you shall kill the woman, and the beast: they shall surely be put to death; their blood shall be upon them.

(Leviticus 20:17)
And if a man shall take his sister, his father's daughter, or his mother's daughter, and see her nakedness, and she see his nakedness; it is a wicked thing; and they shall be cut off in the sight of their people: he has uncovered his sister's nakedness; he shall bear his iniquity.

(Leviticus 20:18)
And if a man shall lie with a woman having her sickness, and shall uncover her nakedness; he has discovered her fountain, and she has uncovered the fountain of her blood: and both of them shall be cut off from among their people.

(Leviticus 20:19)
And you shall not uncover the nakedness of your mother's sister, nor of your father's sister: for he uncovers his near kin: they shall bear their iniquity.

(Leviticus 20:20)

And if a man shall lie with his uncle's wife, he has uncovered his uncle's nakedness: they shall bear their sin; they shall die childless.

(Leviticus 20:21)

And if a man shall take his brother's wife, it is an unclean thing: he has uncovered his brother's nakedness; they shall be childless.

(Leviticus 20:22)

You shall therefore keep all my statutes, and all my judgments, and do them: that the land, whither I bring you to dwell therein, spew you not out.

(Leviticus 20:23)

And you shall not walk in the manners of the nation, which I cast out before you: for they committed all these things, and therefore I abhorred them.

(Leviticus 20:24)

But I have said to you, You shall inherit their land, and I will give it to you to possess it, a land that flows with milk and honey: I am the LORD your God, which have separated you from other people.

(Leviticus 20:25)

You shall therefore put difference between clean beasts and unclean, and between unclean fowls and clean: and you shall not make your souls abominable by beast, or by fowl, or by any manner of living thing that creeps on the ground, which I have separated from you as unclean.

(Leviticus 20:26)

And you shall be holy to me: for I the LORD am holy, and have severed you from other people, that you should be mine.

(Leviticus 20:27)

A man also or woman that has a familiar spirit, or that is a wizard, shall surely be put to death: they shall stone them with stones: their blood shall be upon them.

Leviticus: Chapter Twenty-One

(Leviticus 21:1)
And the LORD said to Moses, Speak to the priests the sons of Aaron, and say to them, There shall none be defiled for the dead among his people:

(Leviticus 21:2)
But for his kin, that is near to him, that is, for his mother, and for his father, and for his son, and for his daughter, and for his brother,

(Leviticus 21:3)
And for his sister a virgin, that is nigh to him, which has had no husband; for her may he be defiled.

(Leviticus 21:4)
But he shall not defile himself, being a chief man among his people, to profane himself.

(Leviticus 21:5)
They shall not make baldness upon their head, neither shall they shave off the corner of their beard, nor make any cuttings in their flesh.

(Leviticus 21:6)
They shall be holy to their God, and not profane the name of their God: for the offerings of the LORD made by fire, and the bread of their God, they do offer: therefore they shall be holy.

(Leviticus 21:7)

They shall not take a wife that is a whore, or profane; neither shall they take a woman put away from her husband: for he is holy to his God.

(Leviticus 21:8)

You shall sanctify him therefore; for he offers the bread of your God: he shall be holy to you: for I the LORD, which sanctify you, am holy.

(Leviticus 21:9)

And the daughter of any priest, if she profane herself by playing the whore, she profanes her father: she shall be burnt with fire.

(Leviticus 21:10)

And he that is the high priest among his brothers, upon whose head the anointing oil was poured, and that is consecrated to put on the garments, shall not uncover his head, nor rend his clothes;

(Leviticus 21:11)

Neither shall he go in to any dead body, nor defile himself for his father, or for his mother;

(Leviticus 21:12)

Neither shall he go out of the sanctuary, nor profane the sanctuary of his God; for the crown of the anointing oil of his God is upon him: I am the LORD.

(Leviticus 21:13)

And he shall take a wife in her virginity.

(Leviticus 21:14)

A widow, or a divorced woman, or profane, or an harlot, these shall he not take: but he shall take a virgin of his own people to wife.

(Leviticus 21:15)

Neither shall he profane his seed among his people: for I the LORD do sanctify him.

(Leviticus 21:16)

And the LORD spoke to Moses, saying,

(Leviticus 21:17)

Speak to Aaron, saying, Whosoever he be of your seed in their generations that has any blemish, let him not approach to offer the bread of his God.

(Leviticus 21:18)

For whatsoever man he be that has a blemish, he shall not approach: a blind man, or a lame, or he that has a flat nose, or any thing superfluous,

(Leviticus 21:19)

Or a man that is broken-footed, or broken-handed,

(Leviticus 21:20)

Or crookback, or a dwarf, or that has a blemish in his eye, or be scurvy, or scabbed, or has his stones broken;

(Leviticus 21:21)

No man that has a blemish of the seed of Aaron the priest shall come nigh to offer the offerings of the LORD made by fire: he has a blemish; he shall not come nigh to offer the bread of his God.

(Leviticus 21:22)

He shall eat the bread of his God, both of the most holy, and of the holy.

(Leviticus 21:23)

Only he shall not go in to the veil, nor come nigh to the altar, because he has a blemish; that he profane not my sanctuaries: for I the LORD do sanctify them.

(Leviticus 21:24)

And Moses told it to Aaron, and to his sons, and to all the children of Israel.

Leviticus: Chapter Twenty-Two

(Leviticus 22:1)
And the LORD spoke to Moses, saying,

(Leviticus 22:2)
Speak to Aaron and to his sons, that they separate themselves from the holy things of the children of Israel, and that they profane not my holy name in those things which they hallow to me: I am the LORD.

(Leviticus 22:3)
Say to them, Whosoever he be of all your seed among your generations, that goes to the holy things, which the children of Israel hallow to the LORD, having his uncleanness upon him, that soul shall be cut off from my presence: I am the LORD.

(Leviticus 22:4)
What man soever of the seed of Aaron is a leper, or has a running issue; he shall not eat of the holy things, until he be clean. And whoso touches any thing that is unclean by the dead, or a man whose seed goes from him;

(Leviticus 22:5)
Or whosoever touches any creeping thing, whereby he may be made unclean, or a man of whom he may take uncleanness, whatsoever uncleanness he has;

(Leviticus 22:6)
The soul which has touched any such shall be unclean until

even, and shall not eat of the holy things, unless he wash his flesh with water.

(Leviticus 22:7)

And when the sun is down, he shall be clean, and shall afterward eat of the holy things; because it is his food.

(Leviticus 22:8)

That which dies of itself, or is torn with beasts, he shall not eat to defile himself therewith: I am the LORD.

(Leviticus 22:9)

They shall therefore keep mine ordinance, lest they bear sin for it, and die therefore, if they profane it: I the LORD do sanctify them.

(Leviticus 22:10)

There shall no stranger eat of the holy thing: a sojourner of the priest, or an hired servant, shall not eat of the holy thing.

(Leviticus 22:11)

But if the priest buy any soul with his money, he shall eat of it, and he that is born in his house: they shall eat of his meat.

(Leviticus 22:12)

If the priest's daughter also be married to a stranger, she may not eat of an offering of the holy things.

(Leviticus 22:13)

But if the priest's daughter be a widow, or divorced, and have no child, and is returned to her father's house, as in her youth, she shall eat of her father's meat: but there shall no stranger eat thereof.

(Leviticus 22:14)

And if a man eat of the holy thing unwittingly, then he shall put the fifth part thereof to it, and shall give it to the priest with the holy thing.

(Leviticus 22:15)

And they shall not profane the holy things of the children of Israel, which they offer to the LORD;

(Leviticus 22:16)

Or suffer them to bear the iniquity of trespass, when they eat their holy things: for I the LORD do sanctify them.

(Leviticus 22:17)

And the LORD spoke to Moses, saying,

(Leviticus 22:18)

Speak to Aaron, and to his sons, and to all the children of Israel, and say to them, Whatsoever he be of the house of Israel, or of the strangers in Israel, that will offer his oblation for all his vows, and for all his freewill offerings, which they will offer to the LORD for a burnt offering;

(Leviticus 22:19)

You shall offer at your own will a male without blemish, of the beeves, of the sheep, or of the goats.

(Leviticus 22:20)

But whatsoever has a blemish, that shall you not offer: for it shall not be acceptable for you.

(Leviticus 22:21)

And whosoever offers a sacrifice of peace offerings to the LORD to accomplish his vow, or a freewill offering in beeves or sheep, it shall be perfect to be accepted; there shall be no blemish therein.

(Leviticus 22:22)

Blind, or broken, or maimed, or having a wen, or scurvy, or scabbed, you shall not offer these to the LORD, nor make an offering by fire of them upon the altar to the LORD.

(Leviticus 22:23)

Either a bullock or a lamb that has any thing superfluous or lacking in his parts, that may you offer for a freewill offering; but for a vow it shall not be accepted.

(Leviticus 22:24)

You shall not offer to the LORD that which is bruised, or crushed, or broken, or cut; neither shall you make any offering thereof in your land.

(Leviticus 22:25)

Neither from a stranger's hand shall you offer the bread of your God of any of these; because their corruption is in them, and blemishes be in them: they shall not be accepted for you.

(Leviticus 22:26)

And the LORD spoke to Moses, saying,

(Leviticus 22:27)

When a bullock, or a sheep, or a goat, is brought forth, then it shall be seven days under the dam; and from the eighth day and there on out it shall be accepted for an offering made by fire to the LORD.

(Leviticus 22:28)
And whether it be cow or ewe, you shall not kill it and her young both in one day.

(Leviticus 22:29)
And when you will offer a sacrifice of thanksgiving to the LORD, offer it at your own will.

(Leviticus 22:30)
On the same day it shall be eaten up; you shall leave none of it until the morrow: I am the LORD.

(Leviticus 22:31)
Therefore shall you keep my commandments, and do them: I am the LORD.

(Leviticus 22:32)
Neither shall you profane my holy name; but I will be hallowed among the children of Israel: I am the LORD which hallow you,

(Leviticus 22:33)
That brought you out of the land of Egypt, to be your God: I am the LORD.

Leviticus: Chapter Twenty-Three

(Leviticus 23:1)
And the LORD spoke to Moses, saying,

(Leviticus 23:2)
Speak to the children of Israel, and say to them, Concerning the feasts of the LORD, which you shall proclaim to be holy convocations, even these are my feasts.

(Leviticus 23:3)
Six days shall work be done: but the seventh day is the sabbath of rest, an holy convocation; you shall do no work therein: it is the sabbath of the LORD in all your dwellings.

(Leviticus 23:4)
These are the feasts of the LORD, even holy convocations, which you shall proclaim in their seasons.

(Leviticus 23:5)
In the fourteenth day of the first month at even is the LORD'S passover.

(Leviticus 23:6)
And on the fifteenth day of the same month is the feast of unleavened bread to the LORD: seven days you must eat unleavened bread.

(Leviticus 23:7)
In the first day you shall have an holy convocation: you shall do no servile work therein.

(Leviticus 23:8)
But you shall offer an offering made by fire to the LORD seven days: in the seventh day is an holy convocation: you shall do no servile work therein.

(Leviticus 23:9)
And the LORD spoke to Moses, saying,

(Leviticus 23:10)
Speak to the children of Israel, and say to them, When you be come into the land which I give to you, and shall reap the harvest thereof, then you shall bring a sheaf of the firstfruits of your harvest to the priest:

(Leviticus 23:11)
And he shall wave the sheaf before the LORD, to be accepted for you: on the morrow after the sabbath the priest shall wave it.

(Leviticus 23:12)
And you shall offer that day when you wave the sheaf an he lamb without blemish of the first year for a burnt offering to the LORD.

(Leviticus 23:13)
And the meat offering thereof shall be two tenth deals of fine flour mingled with oil, an offering made by fire to the LORD for a sweet savor: and the drink offering thereof shall be of wine, the fourth part of an hin.

(Leviticus 23:14)
And you shall eat neither bread, nor parched corn, nor green ears, until the selfsame day that you have brought an offering

to your God: it shall be a statute forever throughout your generations in all your dwellings.

(Leviticus 23:15)

And you shall count to you from the morrow after the sabbath, from the day that you brought the sheaf of the wave offering; seven sabbaths shall be complete:

(Leviticus 23:16)

Even to the morrow after the seventh sabbath shall you number fifty days; and you shall offer a new meat offering to the LORD.

(Leviticus 23:17)

You shall bring out of your habitations two wave loaves of two tenth deals: they shall be of fine flour; they shall be baked with leaven; they are the firstfruits to the LORD.

(Leviticus 23:18)

And you shall offer with the bread seven lambs without blemish of the first year, and one young bullock, and two rams: they shall be for a burnt offering to the LORD, with their meat offering, and their drink offerings, even an offering made by fire, of sweet savor to the LORD.

(Leviticus 23:19)

Then you shall sacrifice one kid of the goats for a sin offering, and two lambs of the first year for a sacrifice of peace offerings.

(Leviticus 23:20)

And the priest shall wave them with the bread of the firstfruits for a wave offering before the LORD, with the two lambs: they shall be holy to the LORD for the priest.

(Leviticus 23:21)
And you shall proclaim on the selfsame day, that it may be an holy convocation to you: you shall do no servile work therein: it shall be a statute forever in all your dwellings throughout your generations.

(Leviticus 23:22)
And when you reap the harvest of your land, you shall not make clean riddance of the corners of your field when you reap, neither shall you gather any gleaning of your harvest: you shall leave them to the poor, and to the stranger: I am the LORD your God.

(Leviticus 23:23)
And the LORD spoke to Moses, saying,

(Leviticus 23:24)
Speak to the children of Israel, saying, In the seventh month, in the first day of the month, shall you have a sabbath, a memorial of blowing of trumpets, an holy convocation.

(Leviticus 23:25)
You shall do no servile work therein: but you shall offer an offering made by fire to the LORD.

(Leviticus 23:26)
And the LORD spoke to Moses, saying,

(Leviticus 23:27)
Also on the tenth day of this seventh month there shall be a day of atonement: it shall be an holy convocation to you; and you shall afflict your souls, and offer an offering made by fire to the LORD.

(Leviticus 23:28)

And you shall do no work in that same day: for it is a day of atonement, to make an atonement for you before the LORD your God.

(Leviticus 23:29)

For whatsoever soul it be that shall not be afflicted in that same day, he shall be cut off from among his people.

(Leviticus 23:30)

And whatsoever soul it be that does any work in that same day, the same soul will I destroy from among his people.

(Leviticus 23:31)

You shall do no manner of work: it shall be a statute forever throughout your generations in all your dwellings.

(Leviticus 23:32)

It shall be to you a sabbath of rest, and you shall afflict your souls: in the ninth day of the month at even, from even to even, shall you celebrate your sabbath.

(Leviticus 23:33)

And the LORD spoke to Moses, saying,

(Leviticus 23:34)

Speak to the children of Israel, saying, The fifteenth day of this seventh month shall be the feast of tabernacles for seven days to the LORD.

(Leviticus 23:35)

On the first day shall be an holy convocation: you shall do no servile work therein.

(Leviticus 23:36)

Seven days you shall offer an offering made by fire to the LORD: on the eighth day shall be an holy convocation to you; and you shall offer an offering made by fire to the LORD: it is a solemn assembly; and you shall do no servile work therein.

(Leviticus 23:37)

These are the feasts of the LORD, which you shall proclaim to be holy convocations, to offer an offering made by fire to the LORD, a burnt offering, and a meat offering, a sacrifice, and drink offerings, every thing upon his day:

(Leviticus 23:38)

Beside the sabbaths of the LORD, and beside your gifts, and beside all your vows, and beside all your freewill offerings, which you give to the LORD.

(Leviticus 23:39)

Also in the fifteenth day of the seventh month, when you have gathered in the fruit of the land, you shall keep a feast to the LORD seven days: on the first day shall be a sabbath, and on the eighth day shall be a sabbath.

(Leviticus 23:40)

And you shall take you on the first day the boughs of goodly trees, branches of palm trees, and the boughs of thick trees, and willows of the brook; and you shall rejoice before the LORD your God seven days.

(Leviticus 23:41)

And you shall keep it a feast to the LORD seven days in the year. It shall be a statute forever in your generations: you shall celebrate it in the seventh month.

(Leviticus 23:42)

You shall dwell in booths seven days; all that are Israelites born shall dwell in booths:

(Leviticus 23:43)

That your generations may know that I made the children of Israel to dwell in booths, when I brought them out of the land of Egypt: I am the LORD your God.

(Leviticus 23:44)

And Moses declared to the children of Israel the feasts of the LORD.

Leviticus: Chapter Twenty-Four

(Leviticus 24:1)
And the LORD spoke to Moses, saying,

(Leviticus 24:2)
Command the children of Israel, that they bring to you pure oil olive beaten for the light, to cause the lamps to burn continually.

(Leviticus 24:3)
Without the veil of the testimony, in the tabernacle of the congregation, shall Aaron order it from the evening to the morning before the LORD continually: it shall be a statute forever in your generations.

(Leviticus 24:4)
He shall order the lamps upon the pure candlestick before the LORD continually.

(Leviticus 24:5)
And you shall take fine flour, and bake twelve cakes thereof: two tenth deals shall be in one cake.

(Leviticus 24:6)
And you shall set them in two rows, six on a row, upon the pure table before the LORD.

(Leviticus 24:7)

And you shall put pure frankincense upon each row, that it may be on the bread for a memorial, even an offering made by fire to the LORD.

(Leviticus 24:8)

Every sabbath he shall set it in order before the LORD continually, being taken from the children of Israel by an everlasting covenant.

(Leviticus 24:9)

And it shall be Aaron's and his sons'; and they shall eat it in the holy place: for it is most holy to him of the offerings of the LORD made by fire by a perpetual statute.

(Leviticus 24:10)

And the son of an Israelite woman, whose father was an Egyptian, went out among the children of Israel: and this son of the Israelite woman and a man of Israel strove together in the camp;

(Leviticus 24:11)

And the Israelite woman's son blasphemed the name of the LORD, and cursed. And they brought him to Moses: (and his mother's name was Shelomith, the daughter of Dibri, of the tribe of Dan:)

(Leviticus 24:12)

And they put him in ward, that the mind of the LORD might be showed them.

(Leviticus 24:13)

And the LORD spoke to Moses, saying,

(Leviticus 24:14)

Bring forth him that has cursed without the camp; and let all that heard him lay their hands upon his head, and let all the congregation stone him.

(Leviticus 24:15)

And you shall speak to the children of Israel, saying, Whosoever curses his God shall bear his sin.

(Leviticus 24:16)

And he that blasphemes the name of the LORD, he shall surely be put to death, and all the congregation shall certainly stone him: as well the stranger, as he that is born in the land, when he blasphemes the name of the LORD, shall be put to death.

(Leviticus 24:17)

And he that kills any man shall surely be put to death.

(Leviticus 24:18)

And he that kills a beast shall make it good; beast for beast.

(Leviticus 24:19)

And if a man cause a blemish in his neighbor; as he has done, so shall it be done to him;

(Leviticus 24:20)

Breach for breach, eye for eye, tooth for tooth: as he has caused a blemish in a man, so shall it be done to him again.

(Leviticus 24:21)

And he that kills a beast, he shall restore it: and he that kills a man, he shall be put to death.

(Leviticus 24:22)

You shall have one manner of law, as well for the stranger, as for one of your own country: for I am the LORD your God.

(Leviticus 24:23)

And Moses spoke to the children of Israel, that they should bring forth him that had cursed out of the camp, and stone him with stones. And the children of Israel did as the LORD commanded Moses.

Leviticus: Chapter Twenty-Five

(Leviticus 25:1)
And the LORD spoke to Moses in mount Sinai, saying,

(Leviticus 25:2)
Speak to the children of Israel, and say to them, When you come into the land which I give you, then shall the land keep a sabbath to the LORD.

(Leviticus 25:3)
Six years you shall sow your field, and six years you shall prune your vineyard, and gather in the fruit thereof;

(Leviticus 25:4)
But in the seventh year shall be a sabbath of rest to the land, a sabbath for the LORD: you shall neither sow your field, nor prune your vineyard.

(Leviticus 25:5)
That which grows of its own accord of your harvest you shall not reap, neither gather the grapes of your vine undressed: for it is a year of rest to the land.

(Leviticus 25:6)
And the sabbath of the land shall be meat for you; for you, and for your servant, and for your maid, and for your hired servant, and for your stranger that sojourns with you,

(Leviticus 25:7)
And for your cattle, and for the beast that are in your land,

shall all the increase thereof be meat.

(Leviticus 25:8)

And you shall number seven sabbaths of years to you, seven times seven years; and the space of the seven sabbaths of years shall be to you forty and nine years.

(Leviticus 25:9)

Then shall you cause the trumpet of the jubilee to sound on the tenth day of the seventh month, in the day of atonement shall you make the trumpet sound throughout all your land.

(Leviticus 25:10)

And you shall hallow the fiftieth year, and proclaim liberty throughout all the land to all the inhabitants thereof: it shall be a jubilee to you; and you shall return every man to his possession, and you shall return every man to his family.

(Leviticus 25:11)

A jubilee shall that fiftieth year be to you: you shall not sow, neither reap that which grows of itself in it, nor gather the grapes in it of your vine undressed.

(Leviticus 25:12)

For it is the jubilee; it shall be holy to you: you shall eat the increase thereof out of the field.

(Leviticus 25:13)

In the year of this jubilee you shall return every man to his possession.

(Leviticus 25:14)

And if you sell ought to your neighbor, or buy ought of your neighbor's hand, you shall not oppress one another:

(Leviticus 25:15)
According to the number of years after the jubilee you shall buy of your neighbor, and according to the number of years of the fruits he shall sell to you:

(Leviticus 25:16)
According to the multitude of years you shall increase the price thereof, and according to the fewness of years you shall diminish the price of it: for according to the number of the years of the fruits does he sell to you.

(Leviticus 25:17)
You shall not therefore oppress one another; but you shall fear your God: for I am the LORD your God.

(Leviticus 25:18)
Wherefore you shall do my statutes, and keep my judgments, and do them; and you shall dwell in the land in safety.

(Leviticus 25:19)
And the land shall yield her fruit, and you shall eat your fill, and dwell therein in safety.

(Leviticus 25:20)
And if you shall say, What shall we eat the seventh year? Behold, we shall not sow, nor gather in our increase:

(Leviticus 25:21)
Then I will command my blessing upon you in the sixth year, and it shall bring forth fruit for three years.

(Leviticus 25:22)
And you shall sow the eighth year, and eat yet of old fruit until

the ninth year; until her fruits come in you shall eat of the old store.

(Leviticus 25:23)
The land shall not be sold forever: for the land is mine; for you are strangers and sojourners with me.

(Leviticus 25:24)
And in all the land of your possession you shall grant a redemption for the land.

(Leviticus 25:25)
If your brother be waxen poor, and has sold away some of his possession, and if any of his kin come to redeem it, then shall he redeem that which his brother sold.

(Leviticus 25:26)
And if the man have none to redeem it, and himself be able to redeem it;

(Leviticus 25:27)
Then let him count the years of the sale thereof, and restore the overplus to the man to whom he sold it; that he may return to his possession.

(Leviticus 25:28)
But if he be not able to restore it to him, then that which is sold shall remain in the hand of him that has bought it until the year of jubilee: and in the jubilee it shall go out, and he shall return to his possession.

(Leviticus 25:29)
And if a man sell a dwelling house in a walled city, then he

may redeem it within a whole year after it is sold; within a full year may he redeem it.

(Leviticus 25:30)

And if it be not redeemed within the space of a full year, then the house that is in the walled city shall be established forever to him that bought it throughout his generations: it shall not go out in the jubilee.

(Leviticus 25:31)

But the houses of the villages which have no wall round about them shall be counted as the fields of the country: they may be redeemed, and they shall go out in the jubilee.

(Leviticus 25:32)

Notwithstanding the cities of the Levites, and the houses of the cities of their possession, may the Levites redeem at any time.

(Leviticus 25:33)

And if a man purchase of the Levites, then the house that was sold, and the city of his possession, shall go out in the year of jubilee: for the houses of the cities of the Levites are their possession among the children of Israel.

(Leviticus 25:34)

But the field of the suburbs of their cities may not be sold; for it is their perpetual possession.

(Leviticus 25:35)

And if your brother be waxen poor, and fallen in decay with you; then you shall relieve him: yea, though he be a stranger, or a sojourner; that he may live with you.

(Leviticus 25:36)
Take you no usury of him, or increase: but fear your God; that your brother may live with you.

(Leviticus 25:37)
You shall not give him your money upon usury, nor lend him your victuals for increase.

(Leviticus 25:38)
I am the LORD your God, which brought you forth out of the land of Egypt, to give you the land of Canaan, and to be your God.

(Leviticus 25:39)
And if your brother that dwells by you be waxen poor, and be sold to you; you shall not compel him to serve as a bondservant:

(Leviticus 25:40)
But as an hired servant, and as a sojourner, he shall be with you, and shall serve you to the year of jubilee:

(Leviticus 25:41)
And then shall he depart from you, both he and his children with him, and shall return to his own family, and to the possession of his fathers shall he return.

(Leviticus 25:42)
For they are my servants, which I brought forth out of the land of Egypt: they shall not be sold as bondmen.

(Leviticus 25:43)
You shall not rule over him with rigor; but shall fear your God.

(Leviticus 25:44)

Both your bondmen, and your bondmaids, which you shall have, shall be of the heathen that are round about you; of them shall you buy bondmen and bondmaids.

(Leviticus 25:45)

Moreover of the children of the strangers that do sojourn among you, of them shall you buy, and of their families that are with you, which they begot in your land: and they shall be your possession.

(Leviticus 25:46)

And you shall take them as an inheritance for your children after you, to inherit them for a possession; they shall be your bondmen forever: but over your brothers the children of Israel, you shall not rule one over another with rigor.

(Leviticus 25:47)

And if a sojourner or stranger wax rich by you, and your brother that dwells by him wax poor, and sell himself to the stranger or sojourner by you, or to the stock of the stranger's family:

(Leviticus 25:48)

After that he is sold he may be redeemed again; one of his brothers may redeem him:

(Leviticus 25:49)

Either his uncle, or his uncle's son, may redeem him, or any that is nigh of kin to him of his family may redeem him; or if he be able, he may redeem himself.

(Leviticus 25:50)

And he shall reckon with him that bought him from the year

that he was sold to him to the year of jubilee: and the price of his sale shall be according to the number of years, according to the time of an hired servant shall it be with him.

(Leviticus 25:51)

If there be yet many years behind, according to them he shall give again the price of his redemption out of the money that he was bought for.

(Leviticus 25:52)

And if there remain but few years to the year of jubilee, then he shall count with him, and according to his years shall he give him again the price of his redemption.

(Leviticus 25:53)

And as a yearly hired servant shall he be with him: and the other shall not rule with rigor over him in your sight.

(Leviticus 25:54)

And if he be not redeemed in these years, then he shall go out in the year of jubilee, both he, and his children with him.

(Leviticus 25:55)

For to me the children of Israel are servants; they are my servants whom I brought forth out of the land of Egypt: I am the LORD your God.

Leviticus: Chapter Twenty-Six

(Leviticus 26:1)
You shall make you no idols nor graven image, neither rear you up a standing image, neither shall you set up any image of stone in your land, to bow down to it: for I am the LORD your God.

(Leviticus 26:2)
You shall keep my sabbaths, and reverence my sanctuary: I am the LORD.

(Leviticus 26:3)
If you walk in my statutes, and keep my commandments, and do them;

(Leviticus 26:4)
Then I will give you rain in due season, and the land shall yield her increase, and the trees of the field shall yield their fruit.

(Leviticus 26:5)
And your threshing shall reach to the vintage, and the vintage shall reach to the sowing time: and you shall eat your bread to the full, and dwell in your land safely.

(Leviticus 26:6)
And I will give peace in the land, and you shall lie down, and none shall make you afraid: and I will rid evil beasts out of the land, neither shall the sword go through your land.

(Leviticus 26:7)

And you shall chase your enemies, and they shall fall before you by the sword.

(Leviticus 26:8)

And five of you shall chase an hundred, and an hundred of you shall put ten thousand to flight: and your enemies shall fall before you by the sword.

(Leviticus 26:9)

For I will have respect to you, and make you fruitful, and multiply you, and establish my covenant with you.

(Leviticus 26:10)

And you shall eat old store, and bring forth the old because of the new.

(Leviticus 26:11)

And I will set my tabernacle among you: and my soul shall not abhor you.

(Leviticus 26:12)

And I will walk among you, and will be your God, and you shall be my people.

(Leviticus 26:13)

I am the LORD your God, which brought you forth out of the land of Egypt, that you should not be their bondmen; and I have broken the bands of your yoke, and made you go upright.

(Leviticus 26:14)

But if you will not hearken to me, and will not do all these commandments;

(Leviticus 26:15)

And if you shall despise my statutes, or if your soul abhor my judgments, so that you will not do all my commandments, but that you break my covenant:

(Leviticus 26:16)

I also will do this to you; I will even appoint over you terror, consumption, and the burning ague, that shall consume the eyes, and cause sorrow of heart: and you shall sow your seed in vain, for your enemies shall eat it.

(Leviticus 26:17)

And I will set my face against you, and you shall be slain before your enemies: they that hate you shall reign over you; and you shall flee when none pursues you.

(Leviticus 26:18)

And if you will not yet for all this hearken to me, then I will punish you seven times more for your sins.

(Leviticus 26:19)

And I will break the pride of your power; and I will make your heaven as iron, and your earth as brass:

(Leviticus 26:20)

And your strength shall be spent in vain: for your land shall not yield her increase, neither shall the trees of the land yield their fruits.

(Leviticus 26:21)

And if you walk contrary to me, and will not hearken to me; I will bring seven times more plagues upon you according to your sins.

(Leviticus 26:22)
I will also send wild beasts among you, which shall rob you of your children, and destroy your cattle, and make you few in number; and your high ways shall be desolate.

(Leviticus 26:23)
And if you will not be reformed by me by these things, but will walk contrary to me;

(Leviticus 26:24)
Then will I also walk contrary to you, and will punish you yet seven times for your sins.

(Leviticus 26:25)
And I will bring a sword upon you, that shall avenge the quarrel of my covenant: and when you are gathered together within your cities, I will send the pestilence among you; and you shall be delivered into the hand of the enemy.

(Leviticus 26:26)
And when I have broken the staff of your bread, ten women shall bake your bread in one oven, and they shall deliver you your bread again by weight: and you shall eat, and not be satisfied.

(Leviticus 26:27)
And if you will not for all this hearken to me, but walk contrary to me;

(Leviticus 26:28)
Then I will walk contrary to you also in fury; and I, even I, will chastise you seven times for your sins.

(Leviticus 26:29)

And you shall eat the flesh of your sons, and the flesh of your daughters shall you eat.

(Leviticus 26:30)

And I will destroy your high places, and cut down your images, and cast your carcases upon the carcases of your idols, and my soul shall abhor you.

(Leviticus 26:31)

And I will make your cities waste, and bring your sanctuaries to desolation, and I will not smell the savor of your sweet odors.

(Leviticus 26:32)

And I will bring the land into desolation: and your enemies which dwell therein shall be astonished at it.

(Leviticus 26:33)

And I will scatter you among the heathen, and will draw out a sword after you: and your land shall be desolate, and your cities waste.

(Leviticus 26:34)

Then shall the land enjoy her sabbaths, as long as it lies desolate, and you be in your enemies' land; even then shall the land rest, and enjoy her sabbaths.

(Leviticus 26:35)

As long as it lies desolate it shall rest; because it did not rest in your sabbaths, when you dwelt upon it.

(Leviticus 26:36)

And upon them that are left alive of you I will send a faintness into their hearts in the lands of their enemies; and the sound of a shaken leaf shall chase them; and they shall flee, as fleeing from a sword; and they shall fall when none pursues.

(Leviticus 26:37)
And they shall fall one upon another, as it were before a sword, when none pursues: and you shall have no power to stand before your enemies.

(Leviticus 26:38)
And you shall perish among the heathen, and the land of your enemies shall eat you up.

(Leviticus 26:39)
And they that are left of you shall pine away in their iniquity in your enemies' lands; and also in the iniquities of their fathers shall they pine away with them.

(Leviticus 26:40)
If they shall confess their iniquity, and the iniquity of their fathers, with their trespass which they trespassed against me, and that also they have walked contrary to me;

(Leviticus 26:41)
And that I also have walked contrary to them, and have brought them into the land of their enemies; if then their uncircumcised hearts be humbled, and they then accept of the punishment of their iniquity:

(Leviticus 26:42)
Then will I remember my covenant with Jacob, and also my covenant with Isaac, and also my covenant with Abraham will I remember; and I will remember the land.

(Leviticus 26:43)

The land also shall be left of them, and shall enjoy her sabbaths, while she lies desolate without them: and they shall accept of the punishment of their iniquity: because, even because they despised my judgments, and because their soul abhorred my statutes.

(Leviticus 26:44)

And yet for all that, when they be in the land of their enemies, I will not cast them away, neither will I abhor them, to destroy them utterly, and to break my covenant with them: for I am the LORD their God.

(Leviticus 26:45)

But I will for their sakes remember the covenant of their ancestors, whom I brought forth out of the land of Egypt in the sight of the heathen, that I might be their God: I am the LORD.

(Leviticus 26:46)

These are the statutes and judgments and laws, which the LORD made between him and the children of Israel in mount Sinai by the hand of Moses.

Leviticus: Chapter Twenty-Seven

(Leviticus 27:1)
And the LORD spoke to Moses, saying,

(Leviticus 27:2)
Speak to the children of Israel, and say to them, When a man shall make a singular vow, the persons shall be for the LORD by your estimation.

(Leviticus 27:3)
And your estimation shall be of the male from twenty years old even to sixty years old, even your estimation shall be fifty shekels of silver, after the shekel of the sanctuary.

(Leviticus 27:4)
And if it be a female, then your estimation shall be thirty shekels.

(Leviticus 27:5)
And if it be from five years old even to twenty years old, then your estimation shall be of the male twenty shekels, and for the female ten shekels.

(Leviticus 27:6)
And if it be from a month old even to five years old, then your estimation shall be of the male five shekels of silver, and for the female your estimation shall be three shekels of silver.

(Leviticus 27:7)
And if it be from sixty years old and above; if it be a male, then

your estimation shall be fifteen shekels, and for the female ten shekels.

(Leviticus 27:8)

But if he be poorer than your estimation, then he shall present himself before the priest, and the priest shall value him; according to his ability that vowed shall the priest value him.

(Leviticus 27:9)

And if it be a beast, whereof men bring an offering to the LORD, all that any man gives of such to the LORD shall be holy.

(Leviticus 27:10)

He shall not alter it, nor change it, a good for a bad, or a bad for a good: and if he shall at all change beast for beast, then it and the exchange thereof shall be holy.

(Leviticus 27:11)

And if it be any unclean beast, of which they do not offer a sacrifice to the LORD, then he shall present the beast before the priest:

(Leviticus 27:12)

And the priest shall value it, whether it be good or bad: as you value it, who are the priest, so shall it be.

(Leviticus 27:13)

But if he will at all redeem it, then he shall add a fifth part thereof to your estimation.

(Leviticus 27:14)

And when a man shall sanctify his house to be holy to the

LORD, then the priest shall estimate it, whether it be good or bad: as the priest shall estimate it, so shall it stand.

(Leviticus 27:15)

And if he that sanctified it will redeem his house, then he shall add the fifth part of the money of your estimation to it, and it shall be his.

(Leviticus 27:16)

And if a man shall sanctify to the LORD some part of a field of his possession, then your estimation shall be according to the seed thereof: an homer of barley seed shall be valued at fifty shekels of silver.

(Leviticus 27:17)

If he sanctify his field from the year of jubilee, according to your estimation it shall stand.

(Leviticus 27:18)

But if he sanctify his field after the jubilee, then the priest shall reckon to him the money according to the years that remain, even to the year of the jubilee, and it shall be abated from your estimation.

(Leviticus 27:19)

And if he that sanctified the field will in any wise redeem it, then he shall add the fifth part of the money of your estimation to it, and it shall be assured to him.

(Leviticus 27:20)

And if he will not redeem the field, or if he have sold the field to another man, it shall not be redeemed any more.

(Leviticus 27:21)

But the field, when it goes out in the jubilee, shall be holy to the LORD, as a field devoted; the possession thereof shall be the priest's.

(Leviticus 27:22)

And if a man sanctify to the LORD a field which he has bought, which is not of the fields of his possession;

(Leviticus 27:23)

Then the priest shall reckon to him the worth of your estimation, even to the year of the jubilee: and he shall give your estimation in that day, as a holy thing to the LORD.

(Leviticus 27:24)

In the year of the jubilee the field shall return to him of whom it was bought, even to him to whom the possession of the land did belong.

(Leviticus 27:25)

And all your estimations shall be according to the shekel of the sanctuary: twenty gerahs shall be the shekel.

(Leviticus 27:26)

Only the firstling of the beasts, which should be the LORD'S firstling, no man shall sanctify it; whether it be ox, or sheep: it is the LORD'S.

(Leviticus 27:27)

And if it be of an unclean beast, then he shall redeem it according to your estimation, and shall add a fifth part of it thereto: or if it be not redeemed, then it shall be sold according to your estimation.

(Leviticus 27:28)

Notwithstanding no devoted thing, that a man shall devote to the LORD of all that he has, both of man and beast, and of the field of his possession, shall be sold or redeemed: every devoted thing is most holy to the LORD.

(Leviticus 27:29)

None devoted, which shall be devoted of men, shall be redeemed; but shall surely be put to death.

(Leviticus 27:30)

And all the tithe of the land, whether of the seed of the land, or of the fruit of the tree, is the LORD'S: it is holy to the LORD.

(Leviticus 27:31)

And if a man will at all redeem ought of his tithes, he shall add thereto the fifth part thereof.

(Leviticus 27:32)

And concerning the tithe of the herd, or of the flock, even of whatsoever passes under the rod, the tenth shall be holy to the LORD.

(Leviticus 27:33)

He shall not search whether it be good or bad, neither shall he change it: and if he change it at all, then both it and the change thereof shall be holy; it shall not be redeemed.

(Leviticus 27:34)

These are the commandments, which the LORD commanded Moses for the children of Israel in mount Sinai.

Final Notes

We hope your journey is enriched and you are blessed through the production of the **Ancient Texts and the Bible** series!

Minister 2 Others would like to hear from you. If you have comments or questions concerning our materials, or if you find errors in our projects, misspellings, or formatting issues. We work hard to provide quality materials, however, sometimes things can squeak by unnoticed. Your feedback is truly appreciated.

We love producing helpful, innovative books and we are grateful for your support! If you have enjoyed this production, please consider writing a review and letting others know about our materials.

If you would like to be updated when we release new books and other materials, please sign up for our e-newsletter on our website.

Thanks!

Minister 2 Others

Minister2others.com

www.ingramcontent.com/pod-product-compliance
Lightning Source LLC
Chambersburg PA
CBHW071808190726
48292CB00008B/2762

9781947751262